Architecture and Model Building

Concepts – Methods – Materials

Alexander Schilling

Concepts – Methods – Materials

Architecture and Model Building

Alexander Schilling

Birkhäuser Basel

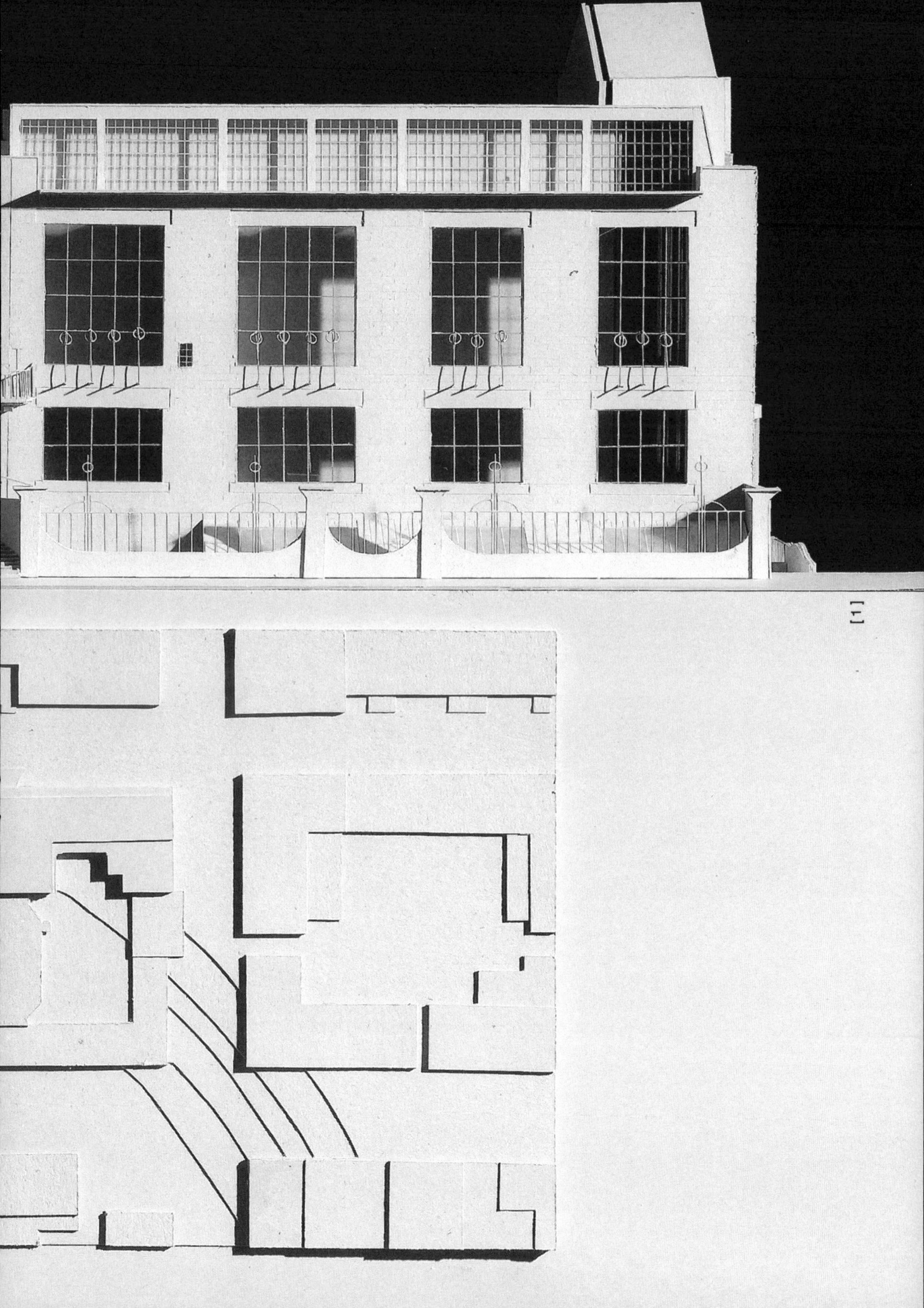

[1]

[1]
Mackintosh Building, Glasgow School of Art, Glasgow, 1897–1909, 1:100, gray paperboard
[2]
Andrea Palladio, Palazzo Chiericati, Vicenza, 1550 1:100, gray paperboard

[2]

Foreword

Every creative process is based on the idea that is present at the start of what is usually the long process of creating a design. This applies in particular measure to architecture, which has been responsible for creating spaces for humans and assigning a diverse range of tasks to the available space in all kinds of original and unmistakable ways right up to modern times. Yet not much has been said concretely or abstractly about precisely how to render the architectural space and objects within that space in terms of perceivable dimensions.

The process of producing architecture should be viewed in accordance with this principle. The processes and methods of creating this architecture evolved in parallel with the architect's profession, which developed from the carpenter's craft in the Middle Ages. How do architects work? How do they develop their products? The oldest and therefore first working tools of the building designer are the drawings showing the floor plans and elevations of the anticipated form and construction of the medieval huts of cathedral stonemasons built on site for the craftsmen to work from during the prolonged construction phases. Almost at the same time, a second, no less important, and – in the truest sense of the word – practical tool emerged, namely, the model.

This book investigates the role of the architectural model as a tool of the architect and examines its possibilities, characteristics, functions and, not least, importance. Next to the final result – namely the completed building – the model is the medium that comes closest to anticipating the built reality. It shares visual commonalities with the building. It is a spatial representation, a three-dimensional object, and can be observed as well as perceived physically or by touch. The important aspects of the space – proportion, structure, materiality, the way it interacts with light, and the resulting character – can hardly be better simulated or depicted than in the form of a model, a miniature version of a visionary architectural object.

[3]
Leo von Klenze, Hans Döllgast, Alte Pinakothek, Munich, 1826–36 and 1952–57
1:100, gray paperboard

[3]

In preparing this book and examining the medium of the architectural model, it quickly became clear that this would be a multilayered subject. The model cannot be defined as occupying a single position in the chain of processes involved in creating architecture, neither in the sense of the people who make the model, nor in the sense of the function it fulfills in representing and communicating architecture. It is much more likely to appear at different places in the designing and building process, and demonstrates the meaningfulness and benefits of its use. On the one hand, it is deeply rooted in the craftsmanship tradition of the model maker, while, on the other, it did not and still does not come about without the architect, who directly and personally needs it as an irreplaceable tool to realize the project.

The discussion starts with the fundamental questions about the theme, i.e., what is an architectural model? Why and for what purpose are models required? And how is a model made?

To better understand architectural models in the context of architecture today, it is essential to look back on the past. What took place in earlier times? How was architecture created, how was a building designed, before there was access to the tools of the digital age, the use of which is now so ingrained and indispensable? Only then is it possible to fully describe and present the current situation in all its facets. The focus of the present study is the roles, uses, and advantages of the model.

Bringing a sequence of actions to a perceivable and defined end is not only a fundamental principle in teaching architectural design. The last part of the book examines the outlook for the model with the question, Where will the built model, the model of the architectural space, find itself in the future?

Alexander Schilling

[4]
This building model clearly shows the patina of time. The black areas are explained by it being temporarily stored in a coal cellar.
Hermann Billing, art gallery, Mannheim, 1907, plaster

Historical Context

1

[5]
Overdoor featuring the relief of the Baroque planned city of Karlsruhe, made in alabaster by Bernd Grimm for the Ungers Archive in Cologne

[5]

Model making today exists within an historical context. For many years – not only in modern times – architecture has been represented in miniaturized form using models as a way of making architectural visions visible and understandable. Earlier generations of master builders greatly appreciated their benefits in expressing their ideas a three-dimensional form.

The earliest evidence of miniaturized depiction of structures can be found in the high cultures of North Africa and Asia. Objects made out of ceramic material depicting buildings have been found in these regions. Few representations of structures in miniature have survived from the period after this time, but the writings of ancient authors such as Vitruvius and Plutarch point to the use of models in the context of building.

[6]

The emergence of the architectural profession

The history of architectural model making is closely linked with the emergence of the architect's profession. The latter manifests itself during the Middle Ages in the masons' guilds of that period and in the exercise of professional crafts such as carpentry and masonry. Master builders were increasingly designing their structures in advance and working less empirically. Surviving from that time are the historic construction drawings on parchment and wooden design study models, which would have been used to assess the effect and the architectural design of the proposed structures.

The wooden model as an expression of the architecture

The Italian Renaissance is the earliest construction era in which architectural models were used to visualize the master builder's idea in three dimensions. All important building works at the time, such as churches, palaces and theaters, were simulated with a great deal of craftsmanship in models made from wood. The model was made as an exhibit for patrons and wealthy employers – a medium for self-advertisement, so to speak. In addition to the usually detailed and artistically produced drawings, the clients had the model as another means of imagining the architecture and were also able to have some influence on the design. The best-known example of this is the wooden model of St. Peter's Basilica in Rome, which was completed over a period of seven years under the leading architect of the project, Antonio da Sangallo the Younger (1483–1546). The purpose of this almost five-meter-high model of the basilica is nothing other than the motives that make a model necessary and worthwhile today. That is, the architectural design needed to be visualized, firstly and in particular to attain a single, cohesive concept despite the frequent changes in architects. The cost of this model was so exorbitant that a real church could have been built on the same budget. Yet despite all this, it is an understandable investment considering the gigantic dimensions of the basilica.

The background and purposes of architectural model making were the same in the Renaissance as they are today. The architect uses the model to communicate; it supplements the drawings with a third dimension and epitomizes the architectural design for the layman. The model becomes the architect's communication medium for the first time.

Model making craftsmanship and materials

The range of available techniques for the manufacture of architectural models was much smaller in the past than it is today. Plaster and wood have been and still are the two most popular materials for model making. The advantages are obvious. As well as everyone knowing how to use them, these materials have good long-term durability.

In the 19th century, the studios of architects such as Hermann Billing (1876–1946) had model making workshops where professional architectural model makers, plaster casters, and sculptors were employed to materialize the historic language of form in plaster and wood.

Circumstances need to have been very fortunate indeed for an architectural model to survive over decades or centuries usually lying protected and long forgotten in architectural and city archives. Relatively few of the great flood of plaster models of buildings and cities of the 19th century have been preserved in construction archives. The purpose of the model is reduced to short-term communication. These objects are hardly ever considered worth keeping for longer. Models stored in the right conditions may develop the noble patina of the originals they were meant to represent just as the full-scale versions change as the years go by. Many models found in archives are "in need of refurbishment"

[6/7]
Strasbourg Cathedral, historic plaster model, probably made in the 19th century, with a timber box for transportation
[8]
Friedrich Weinbrenner and Friedrich Arnold, Local Parliament House, 1820–22, Karlsruhe Model (probably1950) of the building, which was destroyed in the Second World War, painted wood, felt board, plywood mounting board
[9]
Hermann Alker, model of an obelisk, 20th century, plaster
[10/11]
Being paperboard and therefore one of the most rarely conserved types of model, it became collateral damage in the Second World War when it suffered the same fate as the building in which it was archived. It is now kept as a model ruin.
Pestalozzischule, Karlsruhe, 1915, paperboard, wood and sheet-metal

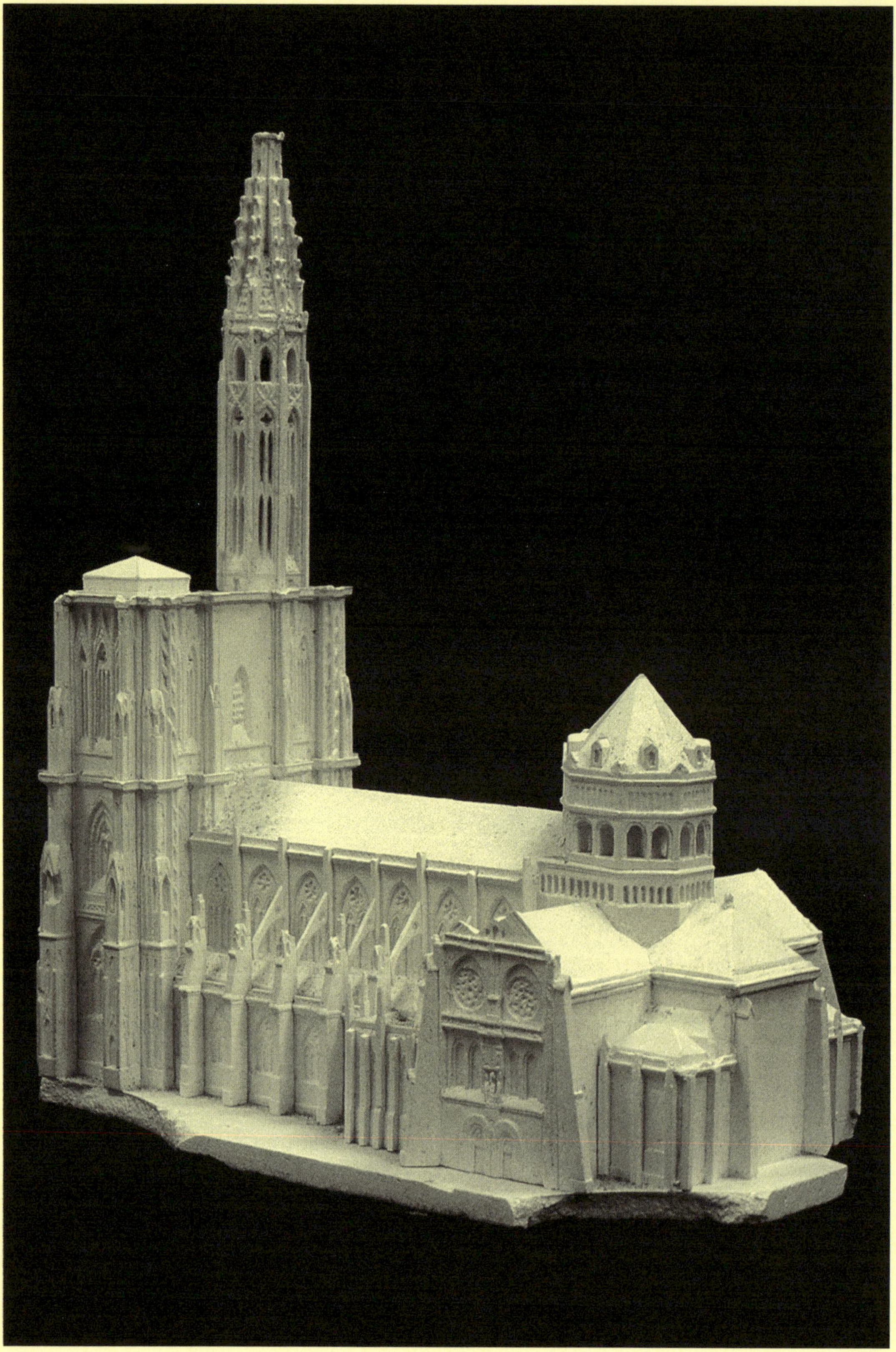

[7]

[8]

[6]

[10]

[11]

[12]

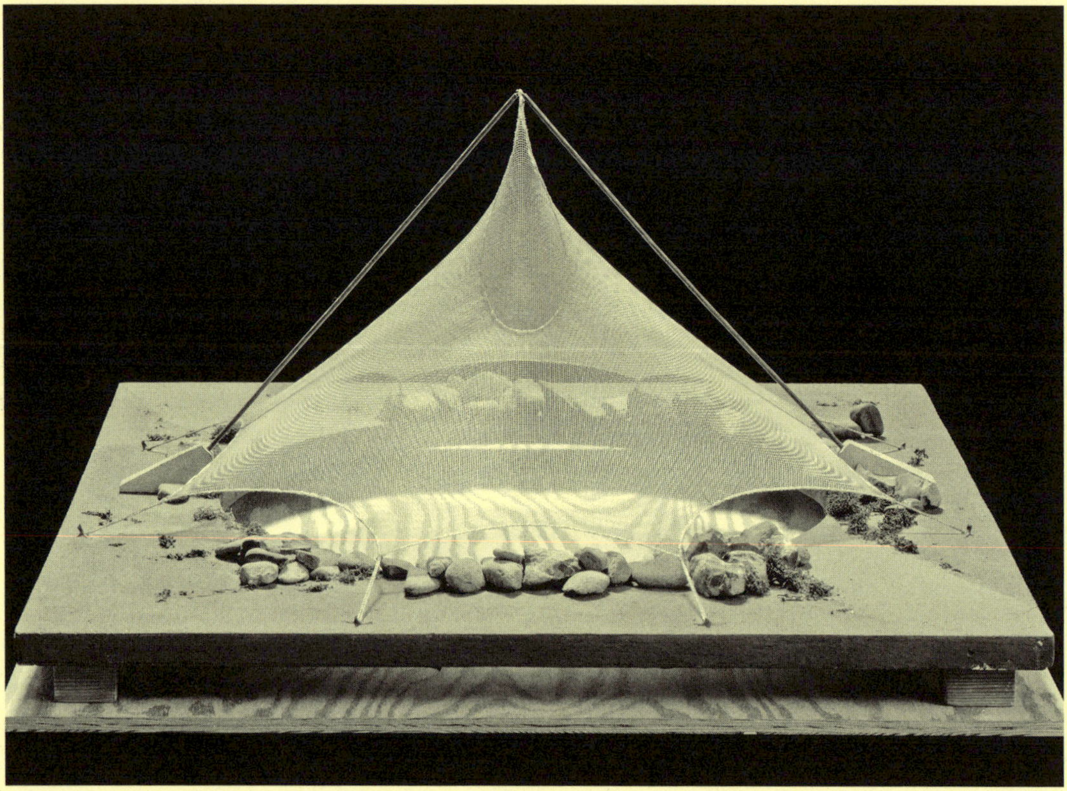

[13]

and show the signs of the passage of time. Archives and museums also contain models that are historic from today's point of view, but are no longer contemporary with what is now their real-world counterparts. From the 18th and 19th centuries onward, models of buildings from earlier periods were made for the purpose of studying or documenting the masterworks of the past.

New materials and new constructions

The 20th century brought a revolutionary momentum to architecture, while technical and constructional advances opened new possibilities and perspectives for building. Propagated in the steel and concrete structures of the 19th century, new styles and developments followed in increasingly diverse forms and at ever-shorter intervals. In the classic Modern Age and the following decades, the methods of depicting architecture – not only model making – were rethought and extended.

During this time, architects further developed the principles of architectural drawing, favoring the use of perspective images over classic two-dimensional sections and elevations. Sculptural architectural models using moldable materials arose. The jump in scale experienced by urban design and architecture in this century can be seen in the larger models of complete urban design ensembles. Technical advances produced fundamental changes in architectural model building. The craftsmanship of the model maker could claim its own place in the context of the design process. Models became increasingly accurate and technically more precise, which was significant for the architectures that they preceded. Because photography was making similar rapid progress, architects used combinations of these two media. With the help of architectural models, perspective photographs were produced in place of the earlier customary analog three-dimensional representations.

In the second half of the 20th century, the model increasingly became the key component of an experimental method of design. Architects lacked experience in working with new construction materials and construction principles. This was overcome by trials and research on analog models. Frei Otto (1925–2015), whose innovative load-bearing and three-dimensional structures had widespread influence on the architecture of his time, was most influential in this field.

[12]
Preserved model of the Jantar Mantar observatory in Jaipur, 1724, India. Only with the help of the model was it possible to empirically determine the precise geometry of the structure and identify its use as a sundial.

[13]
Frei Otto, mesh construction model (with loop), 1964

[14]
Frei Otto, structural model made from rope, 1961

[15]
San Pietro di Montorio ("Tempietto") in Rome by Donato Bramante from the Renaissance, made in alabaster by Bernd Grimm for the Ungers Archive in Cologne

[16]
Presentation model with open sidewall, the model from the Postmodern Age makes reference not only to the architecture, but also to the tradition of the timber models of the Renaissance.
Heinz Mohl, Wohnhaus Mohl, 1983, birch plywood and birch veneer

[14]

[15]

26

Historical Context

[16]

[17]
Hans Scharoun, Schminke House, Löbau, 1930–33, wood, white paint

The Representation of Architecture 2

From historical and present-day perspectives, the model has always claimed a place of its own in the representation and communication of architectural designs. The unique selling point of this medium is that it provides a single or, to be more exact, unique possibility of depicting space in its three perceivable dimensions, namely three-dimensionally, in miniature form. Drawings, sketches and perspectives need the observer to be able to think visually at different levels. Of course, the model is not in competition with the drawing; both are necessary in all phases of a design. On a sheet of paper, the impression of the space is individually formed in the mind of each observer, whereas in the model it is directly readable and can be seen in every case. Nevertheless, the model has one thing in common with all other media of architectural representation – it is an interpretation and abstract adaptation of the architectural idea understood as a miniaturized portrayal and the essence of the built object. As with every medium, the choice of a suitable scale is important for the desired effect.

[18]

The role of the architectural model

Today, the model is usually seen in the context of the architect's actual practice and the design process. In the first place, the model is no more or less than a tool for architects, an instrument for checking their work, which also allows them to recognize and correct errors. The final design never comes about without what may sometimes seem like an endless process of preliminary design, in which the model reveals the potential and weaknesses of the architectural approach without favoring one or the other. In addition to checking the design, the model is irreplaceable for competitions, where different architectural solutions for the same construction project vie with one another for acceptance and have to be compared. Judging the designs is made easier by the three-dimensional display of the building – whether an expression of its urban design context or detailed architecture – which is something the model provides of course. Additional roles are assigned to the model. In university architectural courses during the first semester, young students are made familiar with the experimental approach in every learning situation. They have to try out ideas in order to find the right way to an architectural solution. And this knowledge stays with all architects throughout their whole career. There is no one single way, no obvious way, to satisfy the requirements for a building. The path to a solution is hardly ever a straight line. Architects are (as a rule) no "recidivists," no "repeat offenders" who transfer a proven concept absolutely faithfully in one-to-one correspondence. All architects are, in a certain way, researchers, always seeking the best solution to accomplish the set task.

[18]
Egon Eiermann, Haus Eiermann,
Baden-Baden, 1959–62, model 1:50, wood,
PS rigid foam, painted white

Models and other media for representation

The architectural model is an important working tool in the design process, standing alongside that other essential medium, the drawing.

Architectural drawings and models are the traditional form of representation. This would also include the simple, quick sketch drawn freehand on paper. Spontaneously an idea is given expression on paper and the design process begins, completely naturally, in the time-honored and proven way. Designers seldom express their very first thoughts with a model, because sketches can be done quickly and easily, the ideas being articulated in strokes and lines.

Then technical drawing tools come into play. They may be traditional, such as a set square, triangle ruler, or a drawing pen; or – as is more the rule nowadays – a drawing program on the computer. The results are all two-dimensional design drawings. In every case, a project is represented by several drawings. The use of the plural here makes clear the first difference between drawings and models, namely a number of drawings are required to depict architectural space in its totality.

Analog drawings

Floor plans "numerate" the design in the horizontal projection plane, which by definition is drawn one meter above the floor. Most start out on the principle, demonstrating it graphically and technologically, that the designer lays down the bases in the truest sense of the word for the building. Vertical sections are then prepared, while elevations complete the expression of the building. It is evident, as it has always been, that one drawing alone is not adequate or even simply sufficient to interact with, represent and depict the space. Viewers require all of the individual drawings to exercise their imagination and bring all the information together to form an impression of the whole building. The talent of imagining objects in three dimensions depends on the ability to interpret the drawings and bring the space to life in the viewer's mind. Clients who are not versed in reading and interpreting architectural drawings, for example, cannot recognize the spatial complexity of the design based only on the drawings put in front of them without extra help.

In addition to the simple two-dimensional drawings, there are other means (such as perspective and axonometric drawings) of transferring the

[19]

[20]

[19]
Ludwig Mies van der Rohe, Haus Tugendhat, Brno, 1929–30, model 1:50, paperboard, acrylic glass
[20]
Ludwig Mies van der Rohe, Farnsworth House, Illinois, 1945–51, model 1:50, wood, acrylic glass, painted various colors
[21]
Ludwig Mies van der Rohe, Design for a brick country house, design, 1924 model 1:50, wood, acrylic glass, painted white

[21]

spatial representation from a flat sheet of paper. However, these always depend on the informed decision of the draftsperson in selecting the individual stand- and viewpoint, and therefore are specific to that position. In addition to these analog methods, today also sees the use of computer-supported tools for depicting architecture. Photorealistic or even fantastic renderings in our digital age extend the possibilities by which professionals can communicate the ideas of their architecture to the lay public.

Digital medium – Building Information Modeling

In addition to the traditional architectural model, the word model also appears as part of the term Building Information Modeling (BIM). Here the model is seen as a form of virtual representation of a building. All information is input into a digital model; this includes not only the geometric data developed by the architect but also technical data and all the relevant parameters for the whole design and construction of the building. This results in a bundle of data that describes everything about the building, which everyone involved in the design and construction can access in virtual space. Only part of this complex design tool concerns itself primarily with the architectural representation, namely the digital visualization of the space it generates. The more complex the project and the interfaces, which arise from the multitude of participants, the clearer the usefulness of this virtual model becomes.

However, is the virtual model – insofar as the use of the word model here is correct – in competition with the physical, analog model? Is the architectural model a thing of the past? To answer this question, a brief comparison can be made with music, because, as the philosopher Arthur Schopenhauer said, “Architecture is frozen music.” And how much has digitalization changed the field of music? Synthesizers or computers have not replaced the piano or the organ. Undeniably, a basic phenomenon of progress is that things change and the old is replaced by the new. The new, however, does not necessarily always replace everything that has gone before. It is much more common for progress to open up possibilities. That applies to music. The same applies to architecture, particularly to the methodology of design and construction.

[22]
The dismantlable building model contains all the spatial expressions of the design.
1:100, gray paperboard

Typology

3

An architect's design normally precedes the built reality. Before a building can be erected at a scale of 1:1, a process of design takes place to further develop an idea to the point where it is made concrete. But not every design leads to a built reality, that is, a large number of architectural designs, ideas, and perceptions of the ideal remain visions on paper or in a model. The architect ends up building them only in miniature. An architectural competition, for instance, produces a number of solutions for one and the same design task, and of these solutions, in the best case, only one is built. All other designs disappear into drawers or drawing cabinets and remain visions. Coursework at universities is only a dry run, the sole purpose of which is to communicate that design is a methodical process through repeated exercises, and ensure a new generation is able to take up careers as architects.

In all conceivable design processes, the architectural model is therefore the built formulation of the planned object. If the planned object is realized, the model is its predecessor in miniaturized form. If the planned object is not realized, the model often remains the only token of its existence.

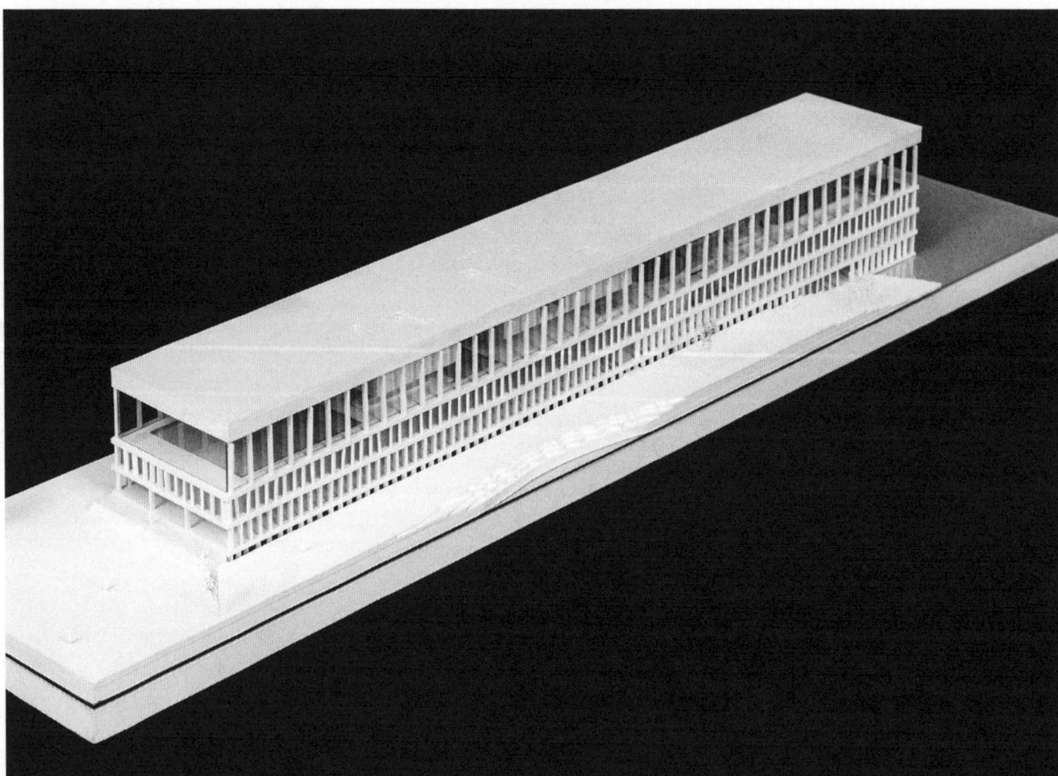

[23]

Scale

Scale is a fundamental term in the specialist jargon of architects, town planners, and many other creative careers. What is meant by scale? What is measured? How is it measured? Is it always "measured"? At the start of their architectural studies, students very soon come across the scale rule, a simple tool with three edges, each with different markings indicating a variety of scales, both large and small. It enables designers to calculate and understand how large a door has to be dimensioned on a floor layout at a scale of 1:100 so that it is shown correctly in relation to all other parts that go into depicting a room or a whole apartment.

When people find themselves thinking deeply and deliberately about the concept of scale, probably for the first time, they realize that the scale of buildings relates to the size of the human body. This human scale becomes internalized and serves as the point of departure for everything to do with architectural design. The size of the human body defines the dimensions of architecture, which is made for people to use. A person is a unit of measurement and the most important reference dimension for the space depicted in the model. The viewer's position and viewpoint are therefore responsible for the perception of the expression that the architectural space communicates.

To be able to design requires an understanding of the scale of objects. How big is an object, a building component or element? Basic activities such as walking, standing, sitting, and lying down, in other words the direct interaction a human body has with architectural elements, likewise form the basis for understanding the principles of scale, such as the proportionality of dimensions. Design is hardly conceivable without a thorough engagement with the dimensions of windows, doors, stairs, floor areas, and heights of interior spaces. In the context of urban space, too, the question of the appropriate scale emerges and re-emerges.

The effect of the model itself depends on its scale. Without scale, it won't work at all. Scale is a means for reality to become miniaturized. The building is depicted at a reduced size. If a wall is 20 meters long in reality, it may be a much more manageable 20 centimeters in the model, which is a considerable advantage in practical terms. Without scale there can be no model. The miniature demands the first decision from the model maker, i.e., how big should it be in relation to reality?

Abstraction

The decision about scale is directly linked with the question of the level of abstraction. If, for example, the building is reduced in size by a factor of 100 – the equivalent of the viewpoint zooming out by the same factor – then details are lost. Items that are responsible for the impression of reality are lost or reduced to the essential.

How is the level of abstraction dealt with in architectural model making? The effects of a three-dimensional reduction in size can be considered as similar to what happens on an architectural drawing. Tiles on a pitched roof are not shown in detail on an elevation. They lose their surface profile and only the essential features are shown, for example vertical lines to explain the fall and flow of rainwater as it drains off the roof surfaces. Windows are reduced to their openings in the wall, while the type and construction of the windows, which are relevant to their later installation in the building, are not shown on the drawing at this stage. This principle can be carried over into the field of model making. The scale determines the level of abstraction, in other words, how real and representational the model appears in relation to reality. A careful consideration of reality is essential for the successful use of abstraction. Abstraction has its effect on all aspects that contribute to the perception of a

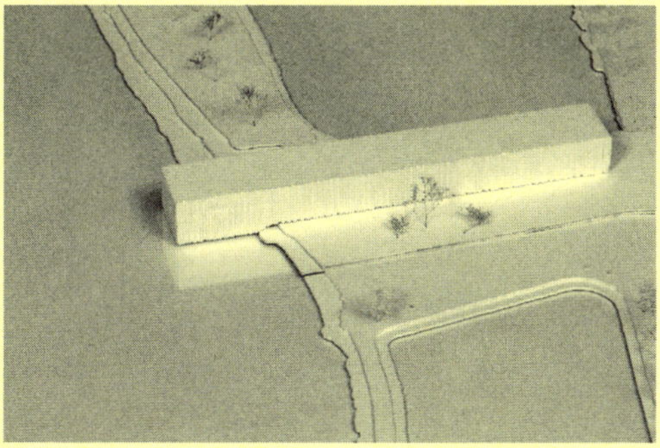

[24]

[23/24]
The abstract urban design model (1:500) shows the building and its mass in the context of its surroundings. The building model (1:200) explains the architectural idea.
[25]
The scale determines the form of representation: the design is reduced to its volumes (1:1 000) or communicates the concrete expression of the architecture (1:200).

[25]

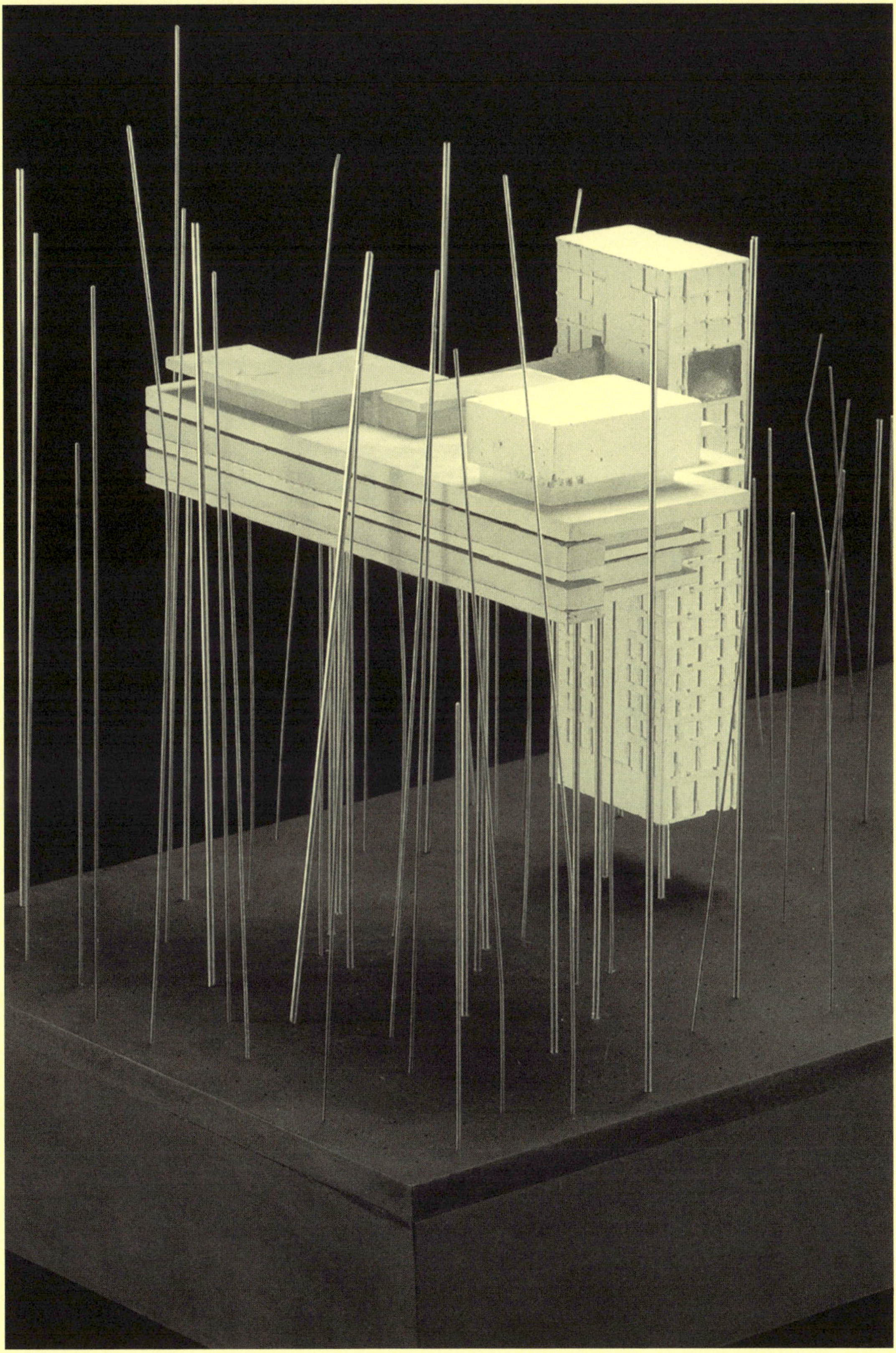

[26]

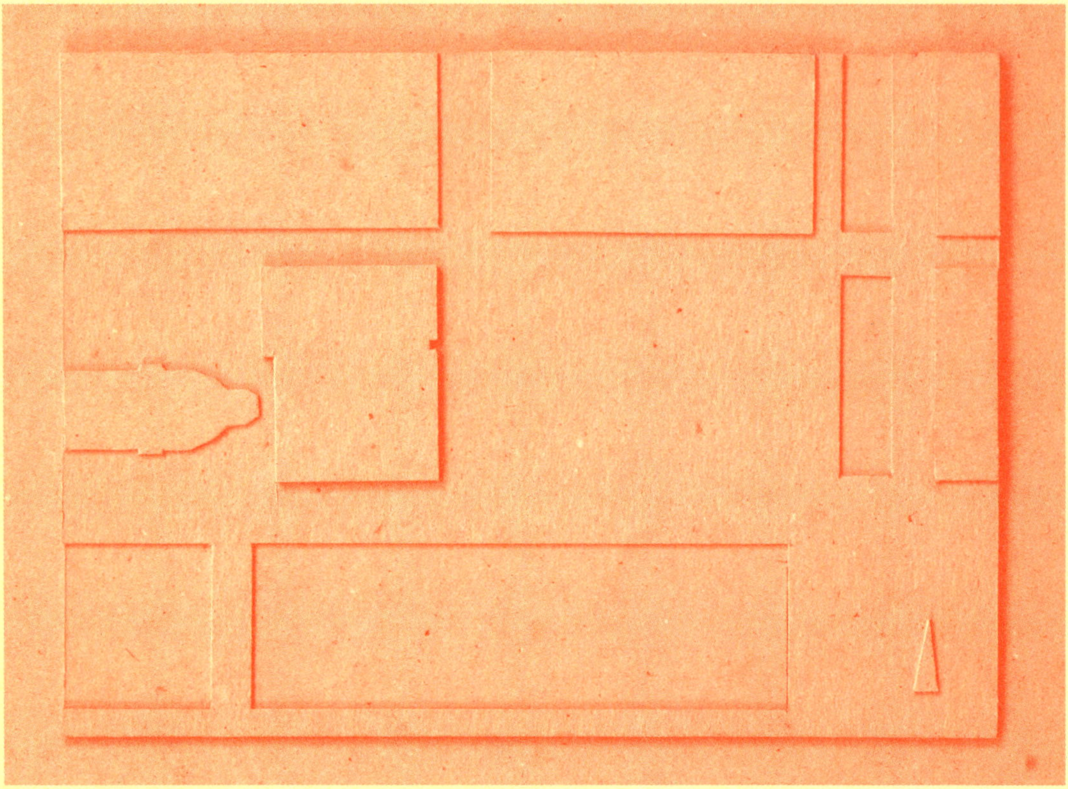

[27]

[28]

building's architecture, i.e., the materiality, substantiality, structure, and texture of surfaces. Impression and character are retained or translated and interpreted in creative ways by miniaturization.

Abstraction and reduction mean that the architectural model must focus on the essence of the architectural design, the spatial and structural expression that the design communicates. This happens not as it does naturally during construction, but requires a logical engagement with the design idea so that the key expression of this idea is visible in the resulting model. At this point, it must be emphasized that an architectural model gives rise to knowledge and not only a finished article. Making the model, that dynamic process of creation involving a huge number and range of decisions, some simple, some complex, serves literally as a model for the final construction process. And significantly so. Model making is the exemplary construction of the building in miniature. The finally constructed building has the same exemplary character as the model at a scale of 1:1, the scale of the built environment and landscape around us. That is to say, the actual design and construction retain an exemplary uniqueness because no construction project is ever repeated exactly with all the same parameters.

[26]
The topography is interpreted abstractly as a negative mass, 1:5000, plaster and brass rods

[27]
Gunnar Asplund, Town Hall, Göteborg, 1934–37. Model 1:1000, gray paperboard. The site plan represents a hybrid of drawing and model.

[28]
Building and landscape in dialog, 1:5000, plaster

Model types

Moreover, the type of model arises either from the design task or the stage in the design process in which it is being used.

The scale information associated with the model type should be considered only as a point of reference indicating the commonly adopted and relative size of each type with reference to reality. The final decision about the scale depends on a wide range of constraints and requirements, not least the pragmatic consideration of how large (length, width, and height) and how heavy the finished model should be.

1. Landscape models and topographical models – scales 1:50000, 1:20000, 1:10000, 1:5000

These types of architectural models attempt to show the landscape surrounding the project at a small scale. They provide a convenient three-dimensional way of representing large natural contexts that will have to be investigated for and will be altered by the proposed project. In landscape architecture and open-space planning, these representations help to analyze and identify the prominent components that shape and define a location. Where the site has a complex surface profile and therefore topographical information is crucial, the model allows the designer to better appreciate the situation. If the model of the existing landscape context is completed before the start of the actual design work, it can be specifically used to depict the existing features of the location realistically.

The highest level of abstraction is found in these models. Ground profiles are usually shown in abstract layers that do not follow the natural, organic shape of a slope, but interpret the desired contour lines on the relevant map as the edges of the layers – an advantage when reading the model and during the construction phase. The layers are stacked one upon the other. Elements that further describe the landscape, such as vegetation, areas of water, and buildings (city and settlement areas and in cases of individual, stand-alone buildings in the landscape), are reduced to their basic characteristics, i.e., vegetation is depicted as anatomized, porous material over the area of the landscape, water as horizontal reflective surfaces, perhaps mirroring the banks, and buildings as simple masses.

2. Site, urban design, urban space models – scales 1:2000, 1:1000, 1:500

At the architectural level, analysis often begins with the context in which the design is to be inserted – a location in urban space, a village or historically developed settlement structure and seldom in a more

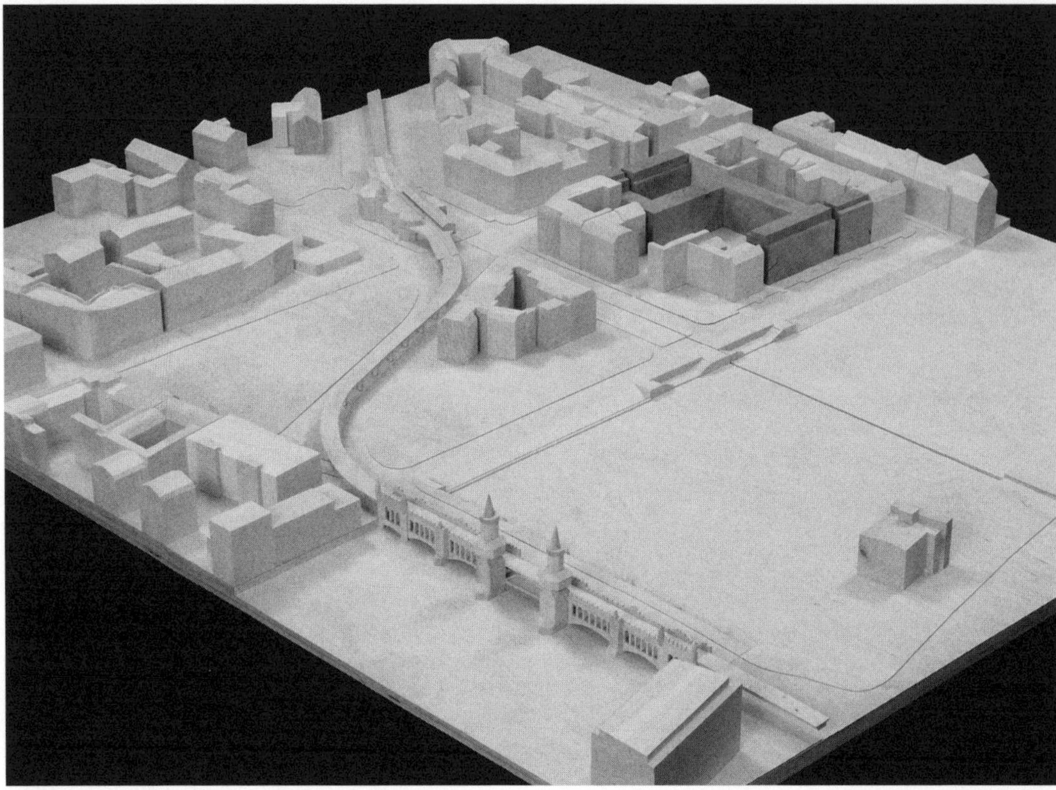

[29]

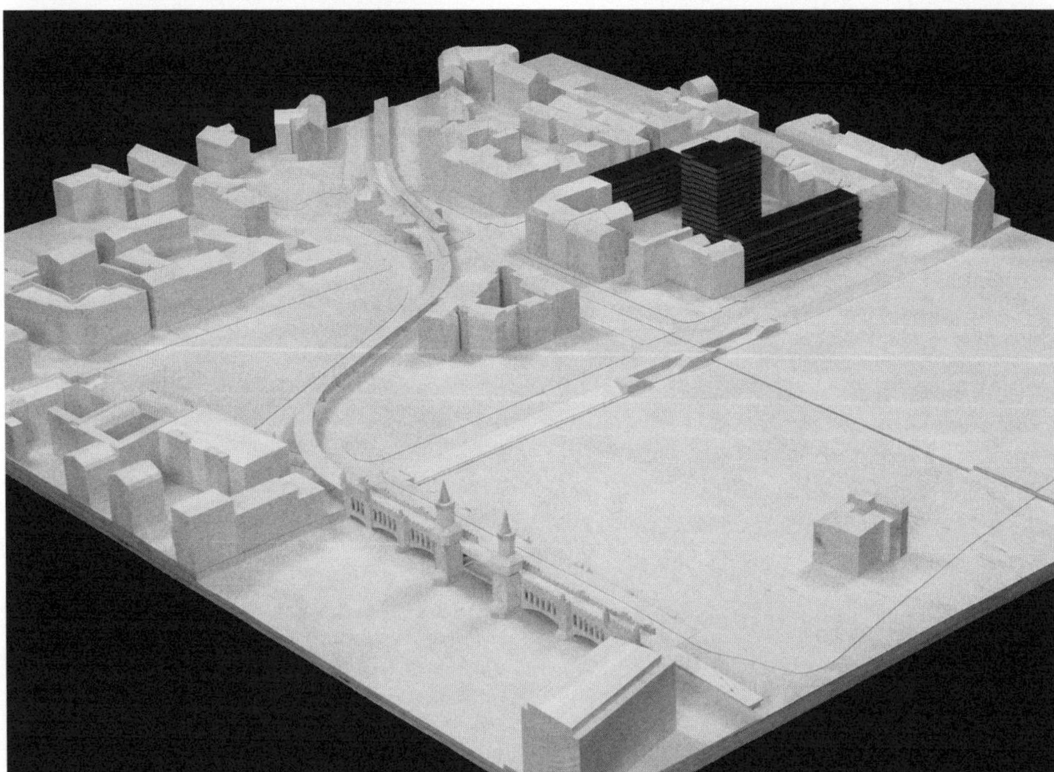

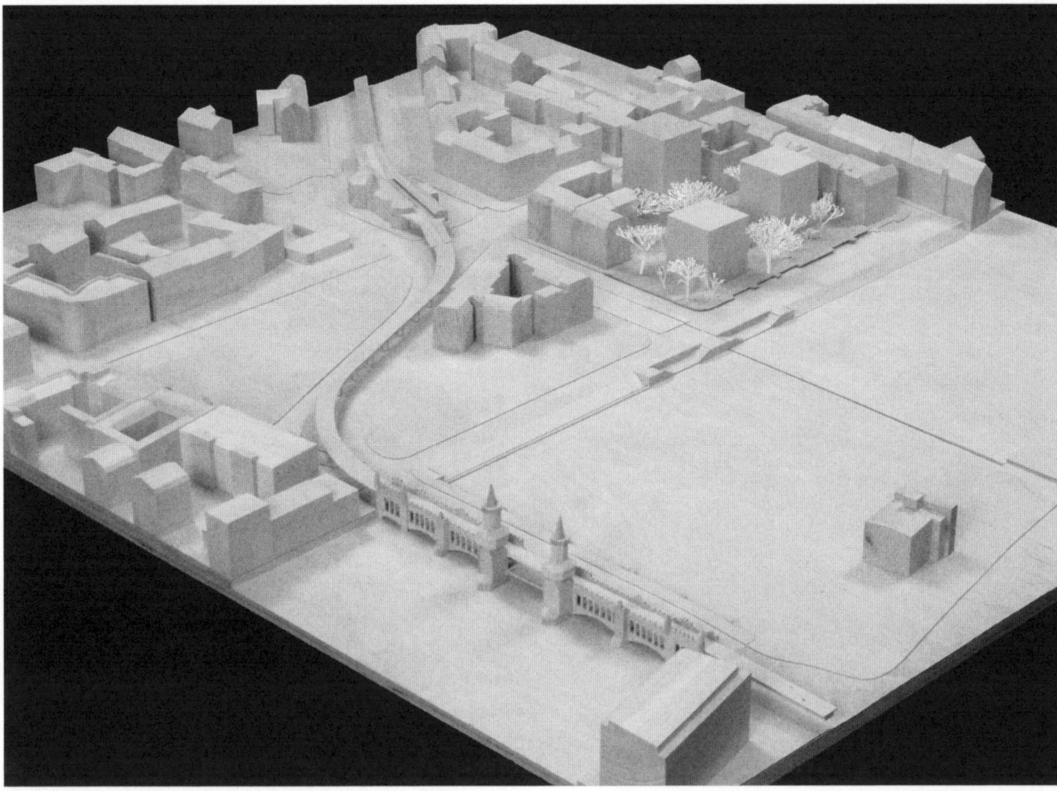

[29]

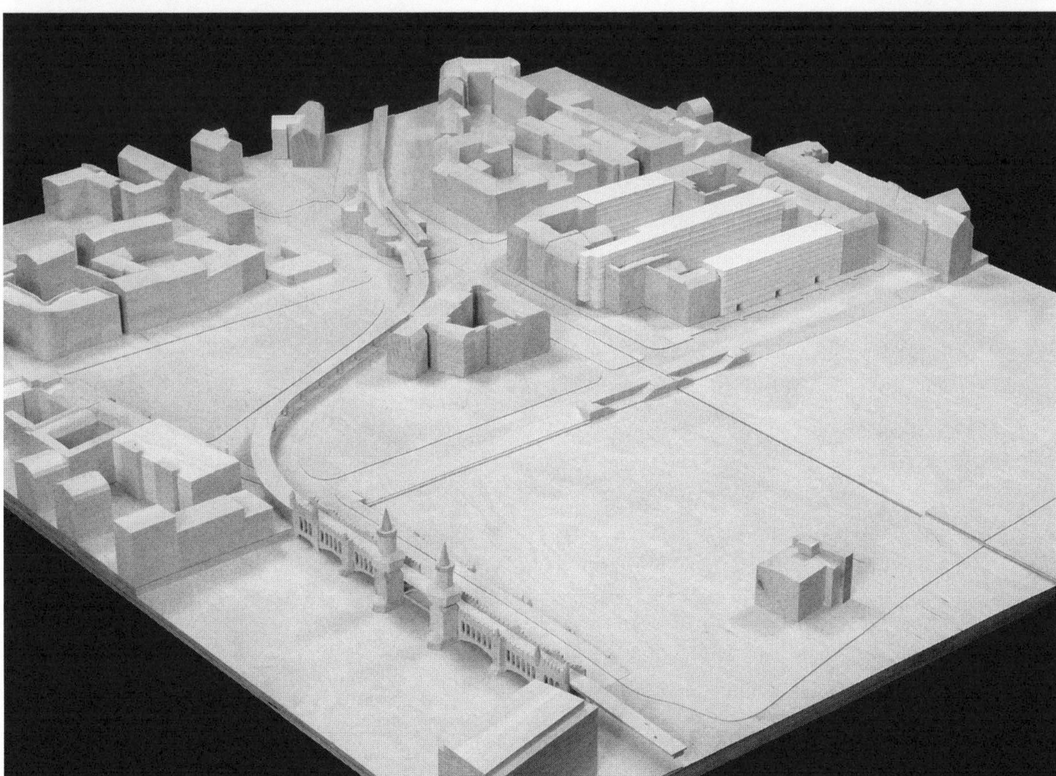

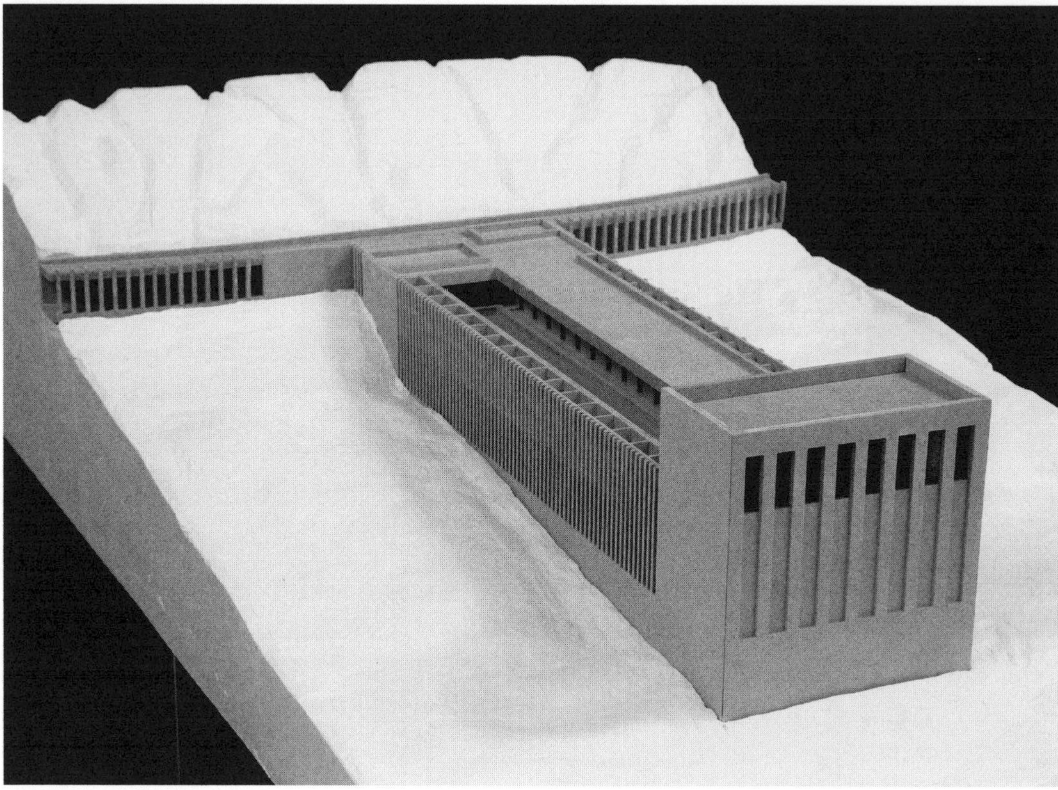

[30]

[29]
City model of Berlin, Oberbaum Bridge – design options, 1:1 000, solid wood, maple
[30]
The composition and proportions of the architectural elements are also expressed in the model.
[31]
City model of Karlsruhe: the three-dimensional pictogram adds other information to the spatial representation.

natural environment or landscape. Designers often work to produce a very real relationship with the existing buildings around the proposed site, while important spatial parameters of the surroundings are analyzed and form the point of departure for the architectural design process. It has proven useful to create a model of the surroundings – normally at a scale of 1:500 – before the design itself begins. The experience of having created the peripheral area around the site once in the model can be extraordinarily helpful in understanding the relationship between the project and the surrounding area, above all if the architect has not had the chance to investigate the site in person due to distance or lack of access.

The model renders important features that define the location much clearer, for example significant roof projections on buildings, or homogeneous structures and textures of facades and other surfaces. "Strategic" objectives, however, are not lost from view because the environment is given a voice in terms of its character, but also stands in relation to the represented design in the same way an orchestra sits with its soloist in the foreground (see Fig. 36).

Most projects will use not just one scale to explain the design, but two or three models at different scales to express different aspects:

Level of explanation

1. The context (of the surroundings)
2. The design (of the building)
3. The focus (on the detail)

3. Building models – scales 1:200, 1:100, 1:50

The first thing an architectural model brings to mind is a model of a building. There are many ways to define and represent architecture in the model and, not surprisingly, the building as a whole is the most frequent subject of an architectural model. At the scales mentioned above, it is possible to interpret and systematize all the architectural elements that make the design unique. In these models, the context is no longer in the foreground of the expression, the building itself is considered under the following important criteria:

Architectural form

1. Scale and dimensional accuracy
2. Articulation
3. Composition
4. Proportions – relationship of the elements one to another

Structure – the principles of construction:

1. Volumetric approach (masses and voids)
2. Walls and ceilings as panels and slabs
3. Stud walling and framed construction
4. Lightweight room-defining elements

Every design requires a choice to be made about the construction of the architectural model. Should the model represent the building in its entirety in order to communicate the expression of the building in the best possible way, or can the information that the model conveys be revealed in a number of layers? At these sorts of scales, it is quite easy not to permanently attach all parts of the building together and instead take a modular approach and design it to be dismantled to make the architect's thoughts and the building's use clear. This could be done with, for example, removable roofs, walls or complete building units and whole stories.

The sectional model is a special version of a building model, displaying only half the structure. It is worthwhile showing the model in section and not only for symmetrically designed buildings. Half a building may well be enough on the understanding that the building is symmetrical, but it can also be useful, like a three-dimensional section on a

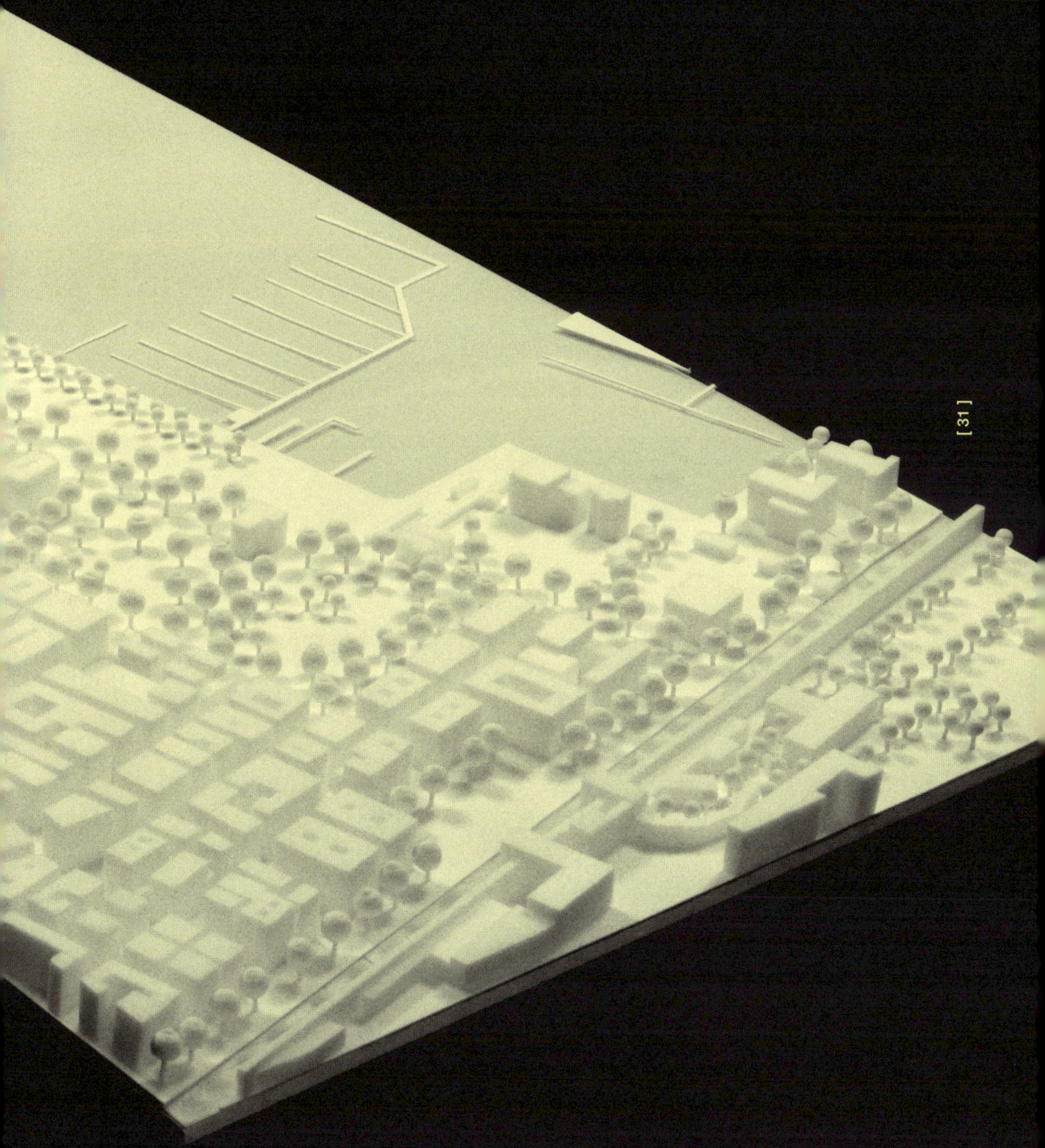

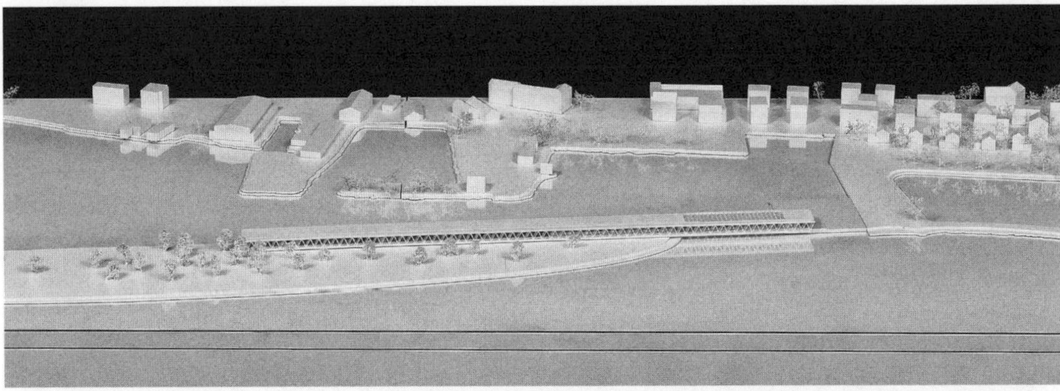

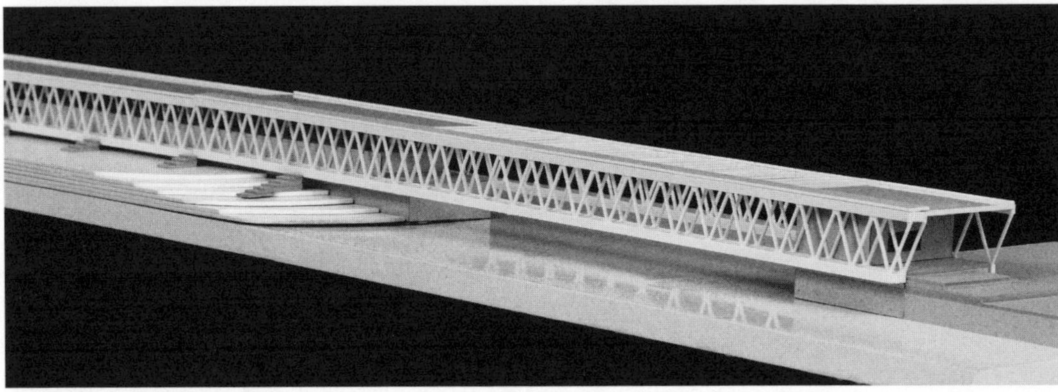

[32]

[33]

[34]

[31]
City model of La Spezia with harbor/ coast. Design on water, 1:1 000, color highlights

[32]
The models guide the viewer‘s eyes from consideration of the whole to the significant detail. 1:500 → 1:200 → 1:20

[33/34]
The type of model determines the interpretation of the design in relation to the urban surroundings and the architecture. 1:500 → 1:100

[35]
The dismantlable building model contains all the spatial expressions of the design. 1:100, gray paperboard

[36]
The monochrome model focuses on the expression of the architectural form.

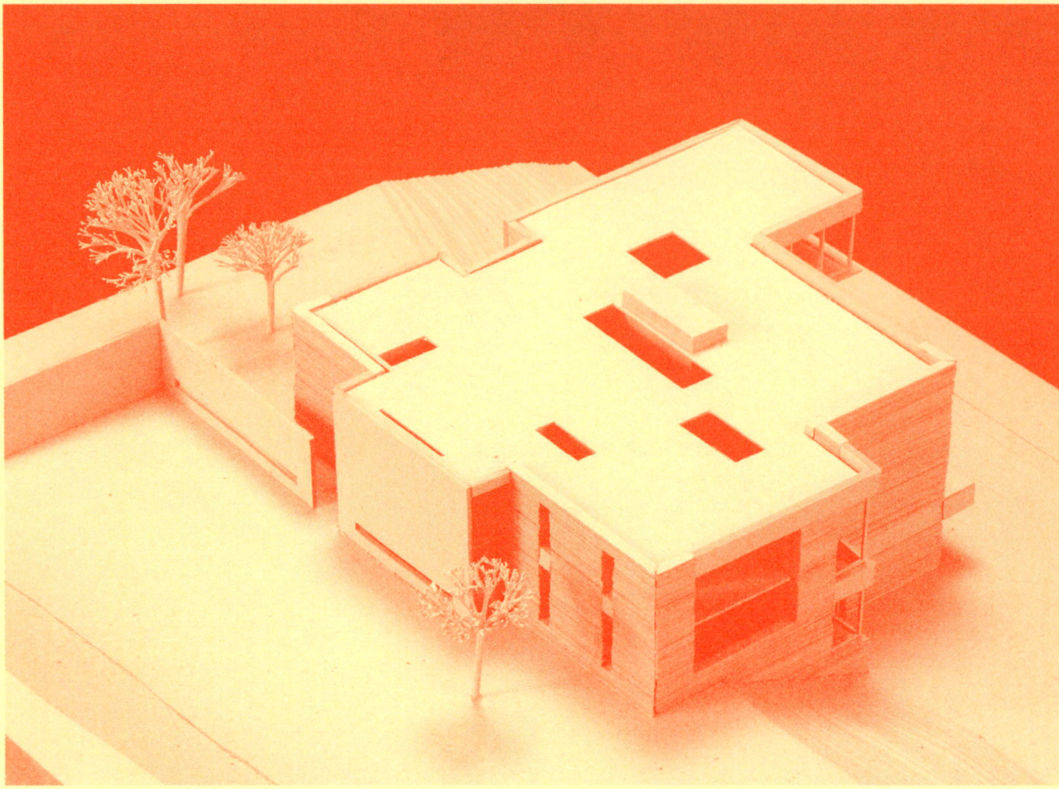

50

Typology

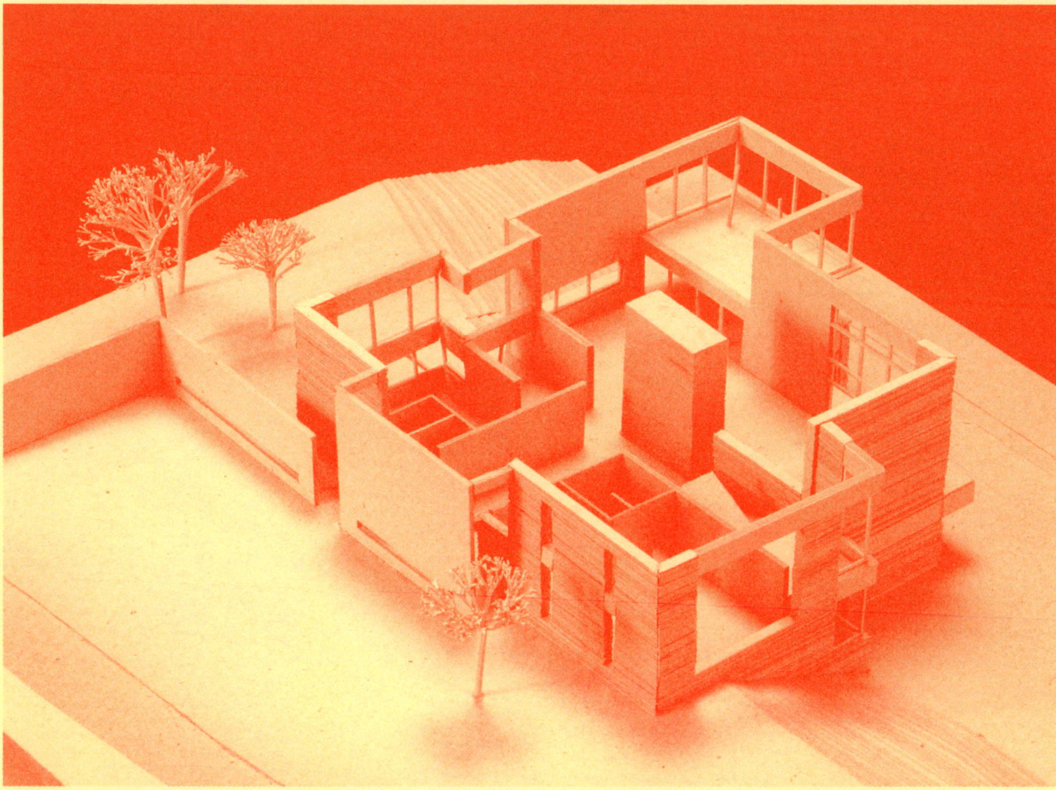

[35]

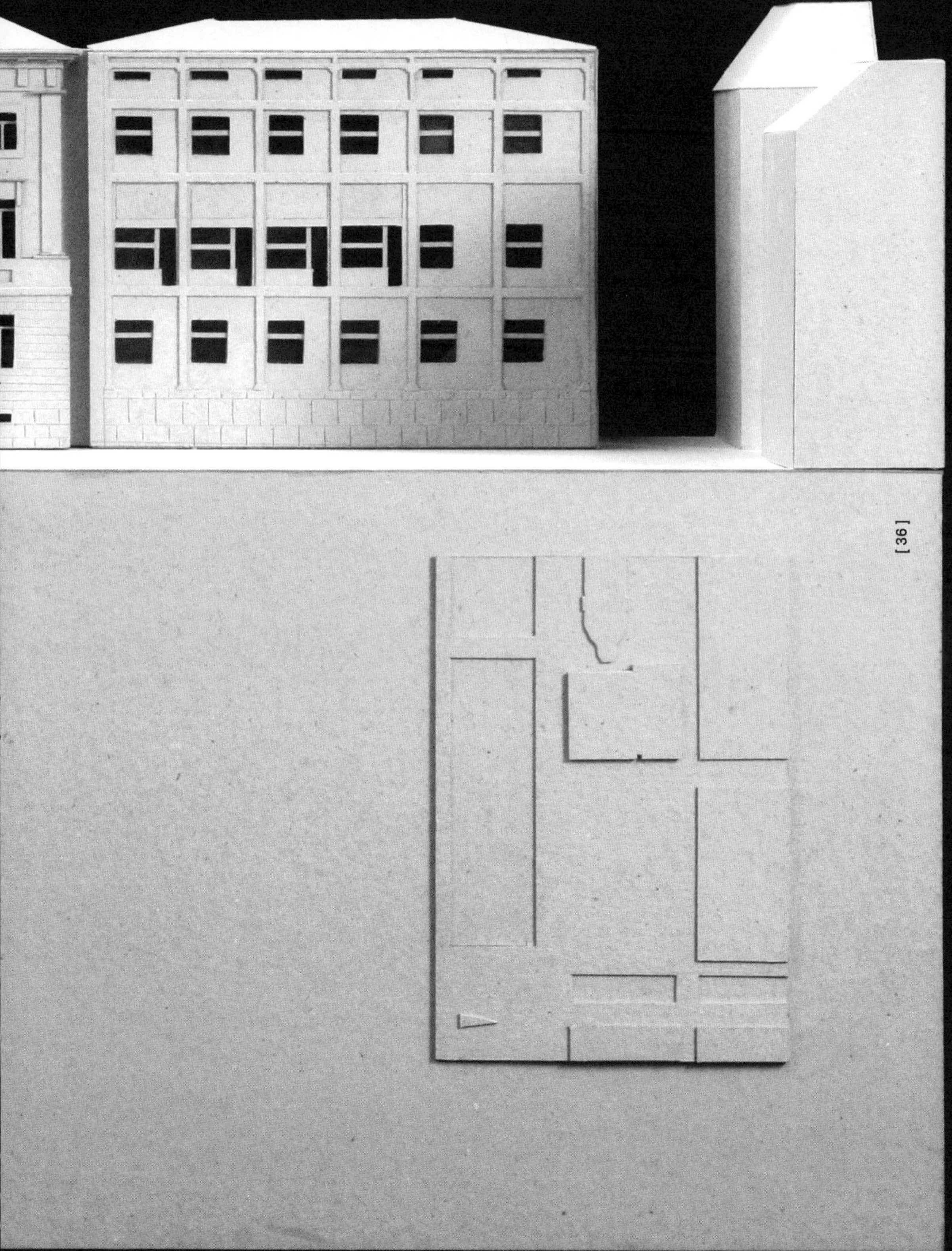

[36]

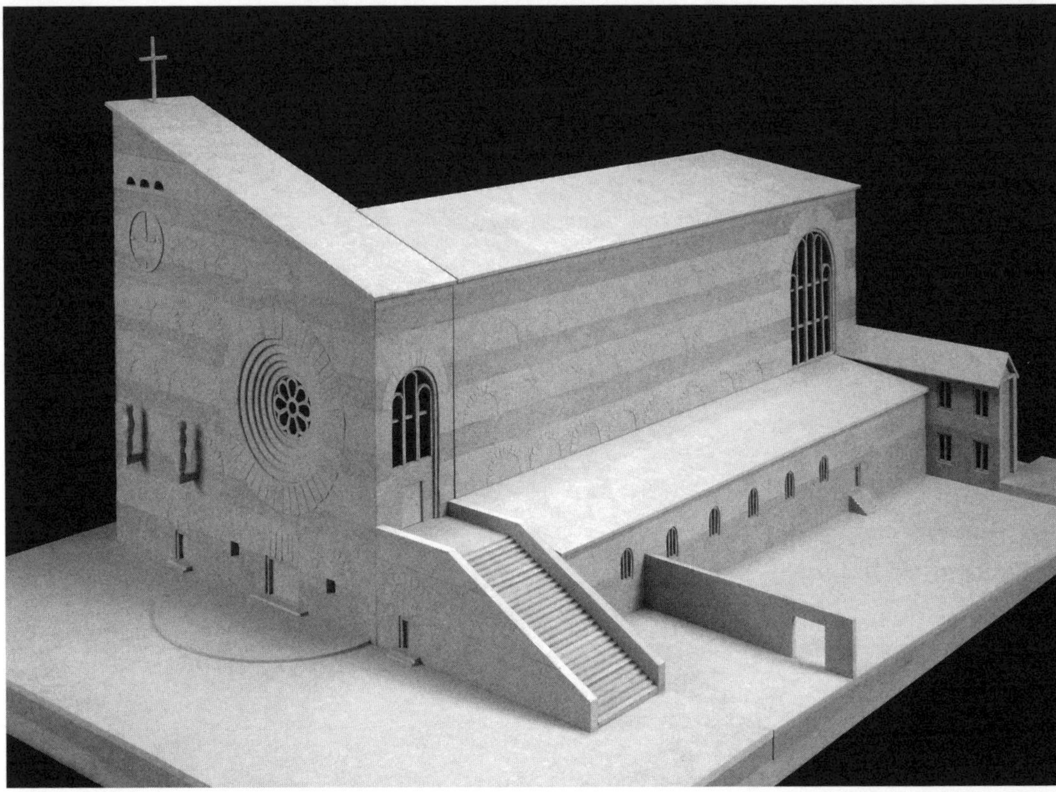

[37]

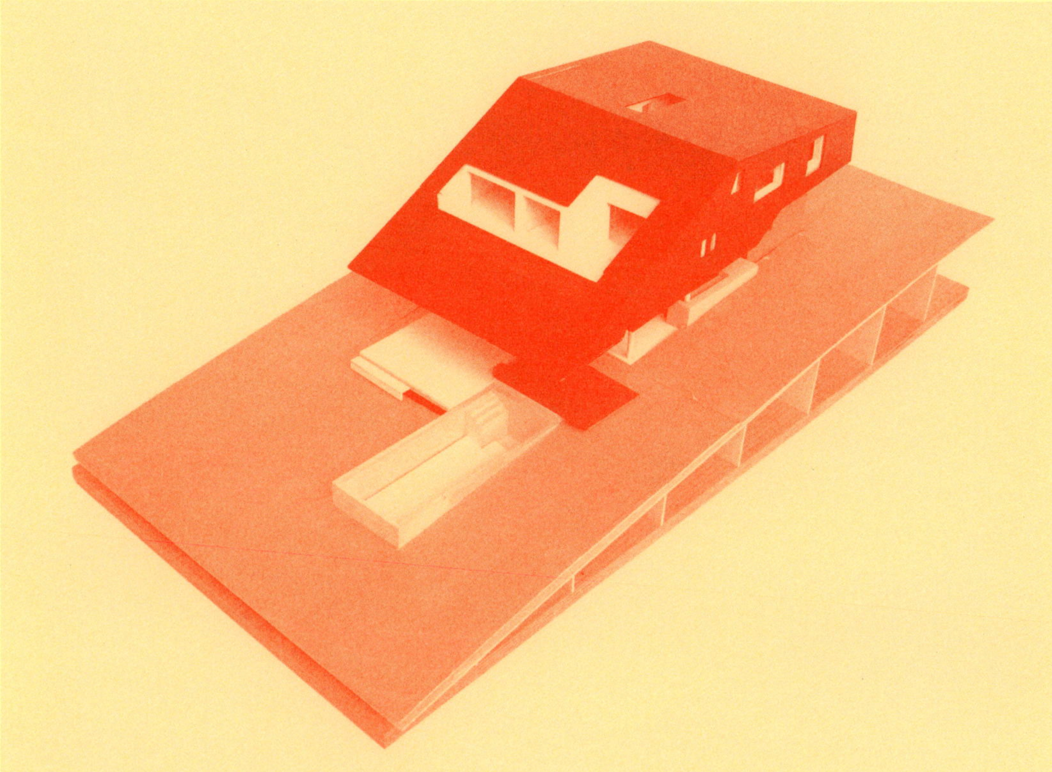

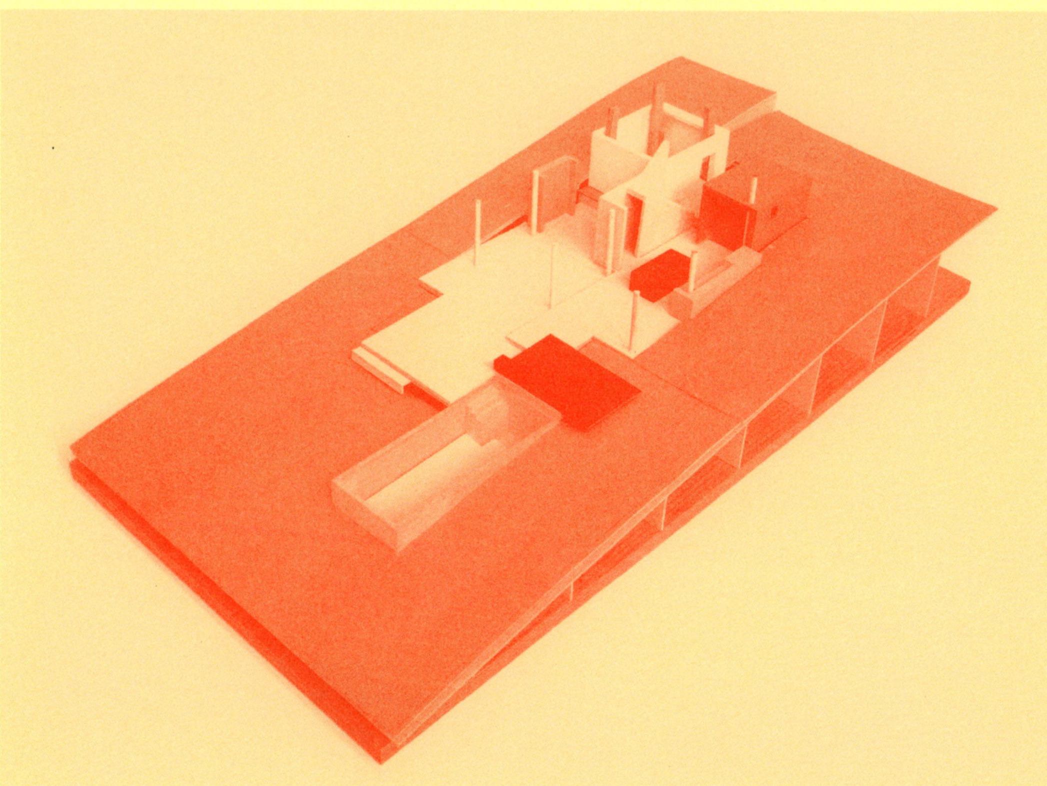

[38]

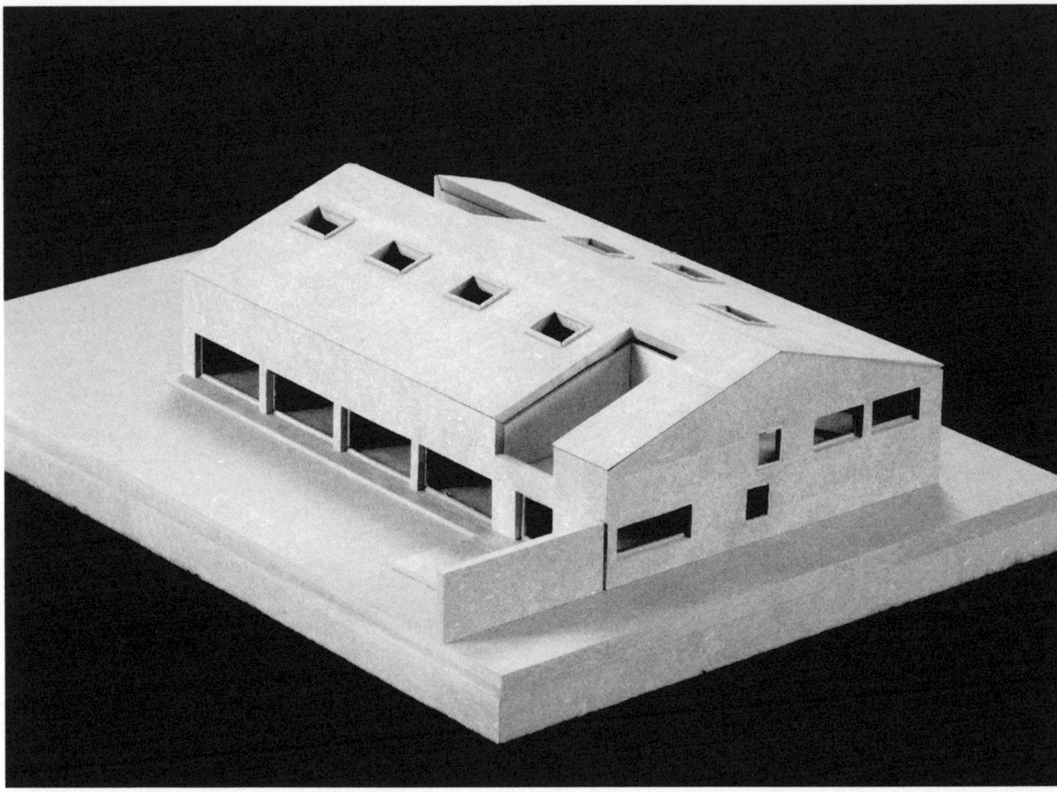

[39]

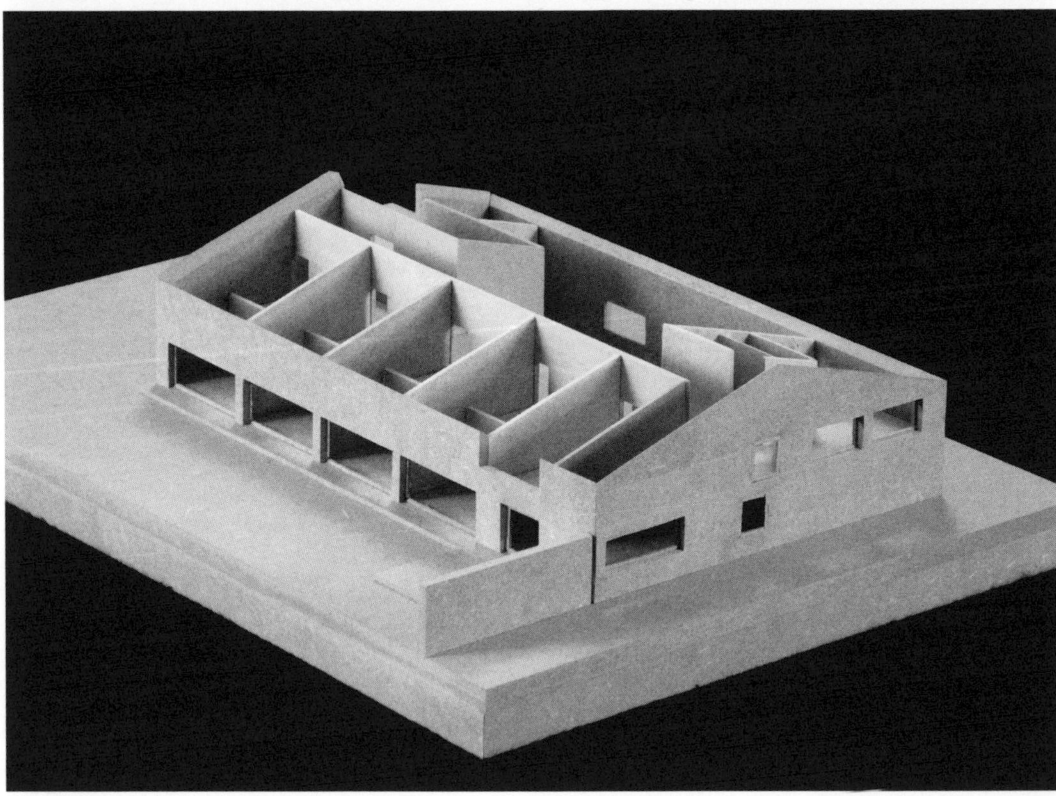

Materiality – surfaces and their characteristic forms of expression:

1. Rough and rugged surfaces
2. Hard surfaces with precise edges and corners
3. Soft and delicately proportioned surfaces
3. Formed, organic, and amorphous surfaces
4. A material's own color
5. The effect of light – absorption and reflection

[40]

drawing, to explain aspects of the spatial depth of any building. However, if the complete building is of interest to the viewer, a mirror can be made to measure for the model and is a clever trick to avoid having to make an identical half-building.

A sectional model that completely cuts through the building to reveal the principles of the interior space gives the viewer the opportunity to look inside. The arrangement of the individual rooms and interior spaces inside the building can be interpreted in this type of representation, as can vertical elements extending over several floors, for example stairs and circulation routes.

The structural model is a further variant of the model type that reduces the building to its shell. By leaving out the final form-giving parts (building envelope, some internal walls and attached components), a building model can represent the basic structure of the design. It is particularly useful to use this form of representation to communicate the principle of building types in which the design is derived largely from its load-bearing structure. The later overall architectural shape can either be interpreted in another model so that the structural model serves as an example of the building shell, while the later model represents what could be called the external fitting out. It may be that the intended form of articulation of the parts makes it possible to incorporate these in a single model. In this case, the building model functions like a series of additive modules in which the parts can be put together loosely to be displayed in the dismantled or assembled state.

The structural models are targeted less at the clients than at specialist designers, such as the structural or building services engineers, to facilitate discussion of construction and technical

[37]
From the urban design model to the building model, 1:500 → 1:100

[38]
By using different colors, the architectural concept and above all the articulation of the architectural elements with one another are made clear. 1:50, paperboard in various colors

[39]
The building model is reduced to the room-defining walls and ceilings. 1:50, MDF

[40]
The removable roof reveals the load-bearing system. 1:50

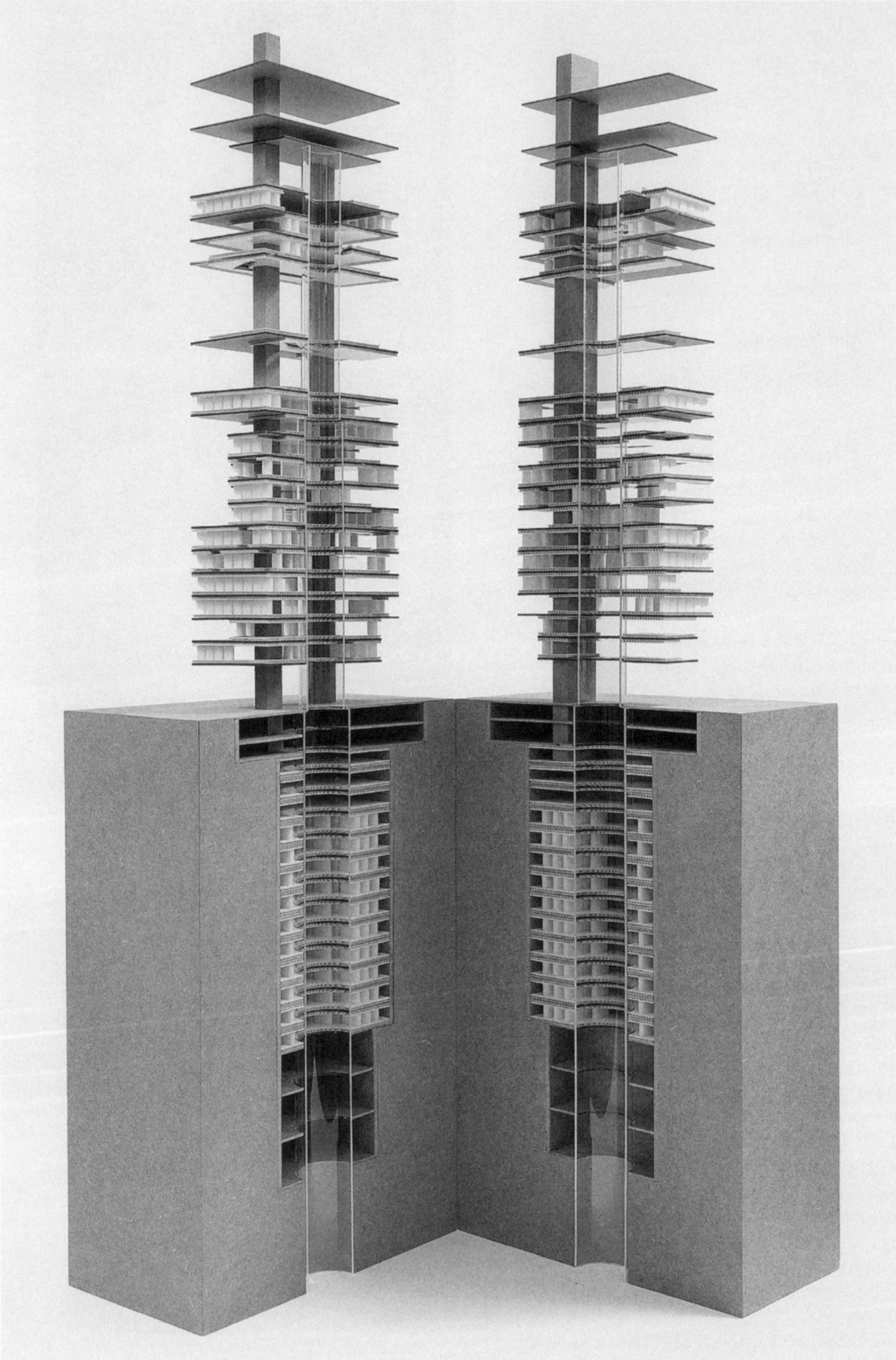

58

Typology

[41]

[42]

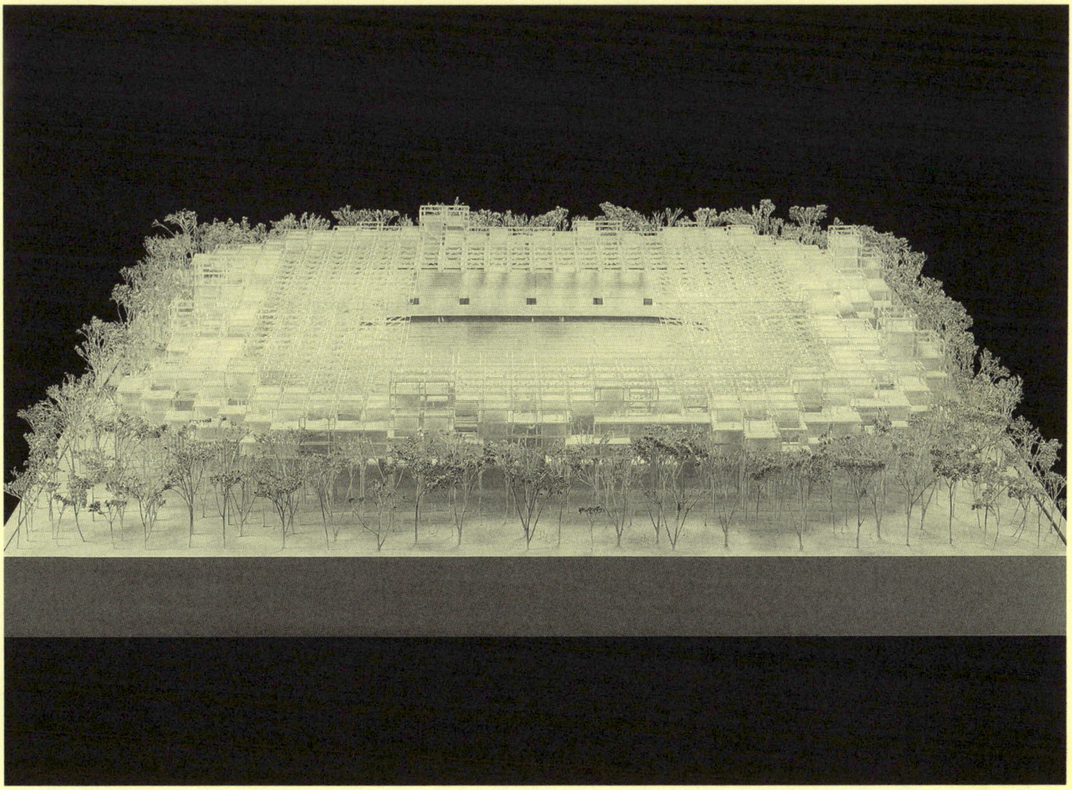

[43]

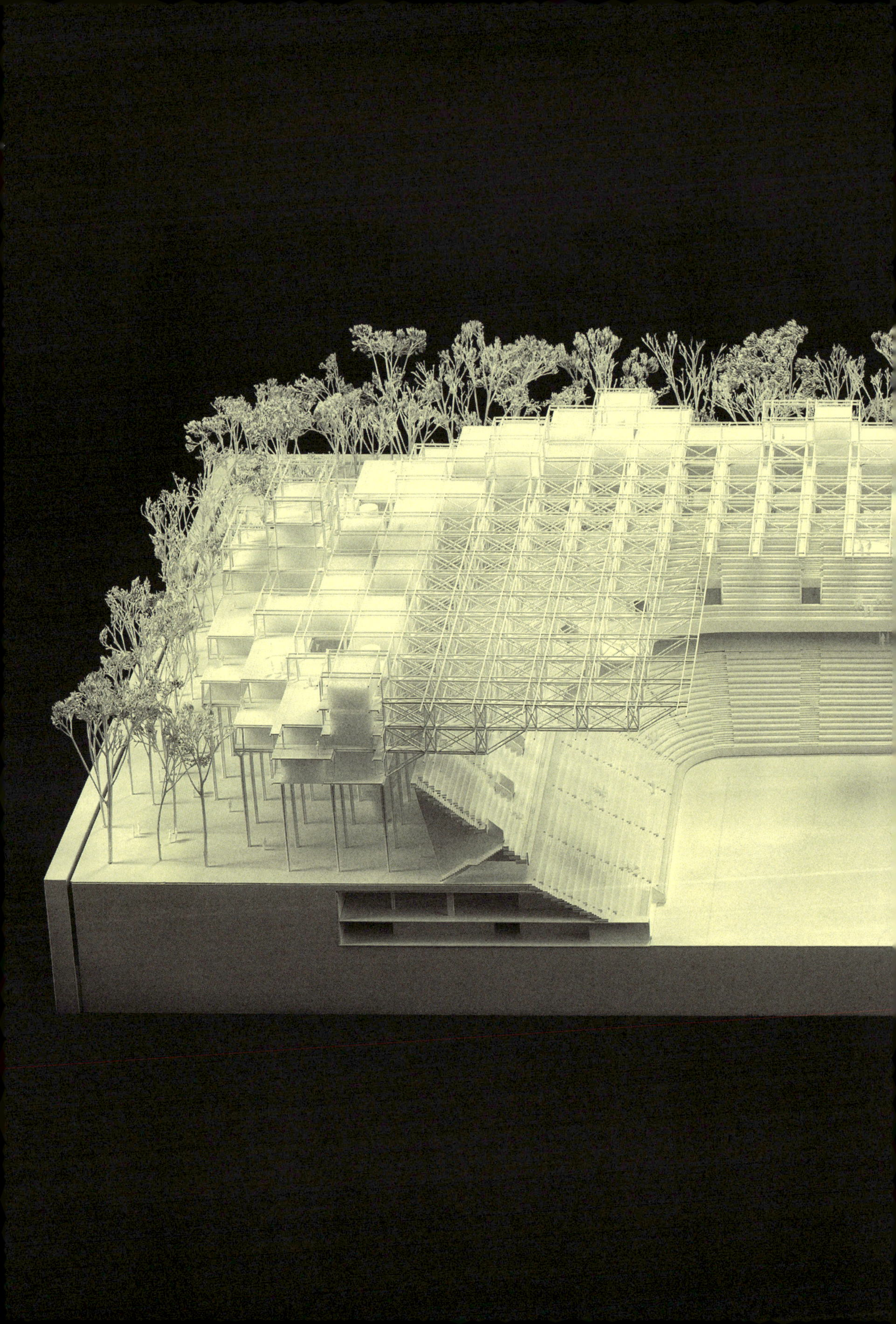

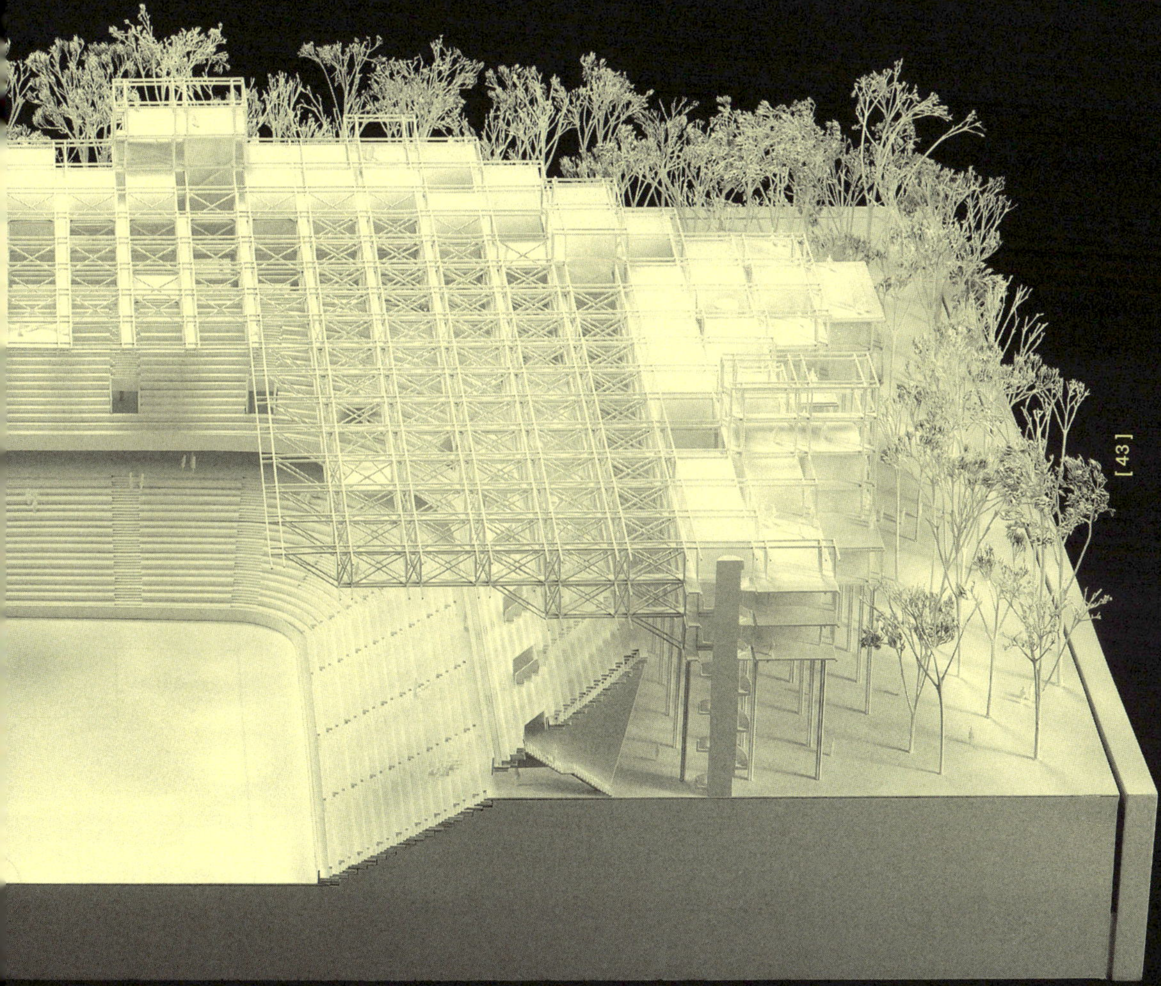

[43]

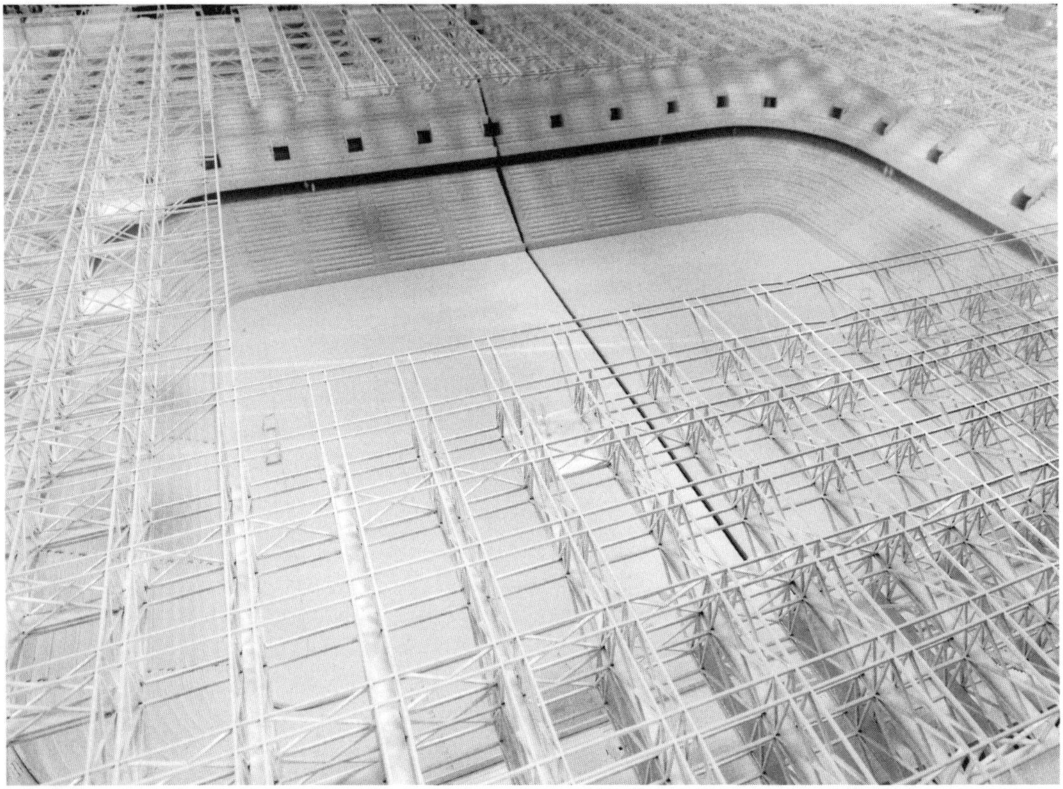

[44]

[41]
Both fold-out models show the spatial arrangement of the interior design in section.
[42]
The vertically cut-through building reveals its interior.
[43]
Building types such as sports stadiums are perfect for representation using symmetrically cut sectional models because they allow a good view of all the internal details.
[44]
The building is shown here without its envelope to reveal the load-bearing structure.
[45]
The design is defined by the building's load-bearing structure.
[46]
A building model cut through horizontally opens up the possibility of giving a third dimension to the horizontal cross section on the drawing.

[45]

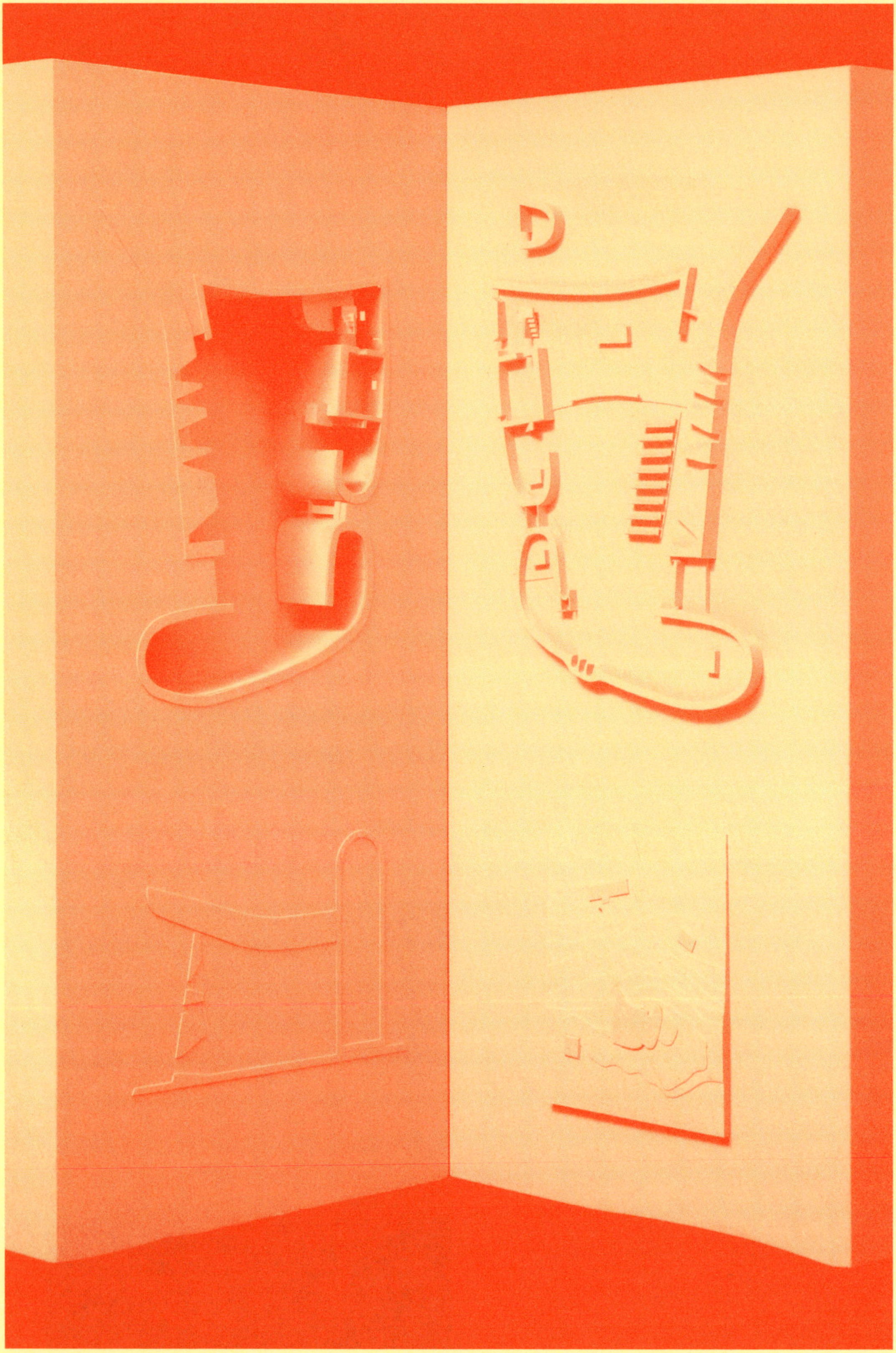

[46]

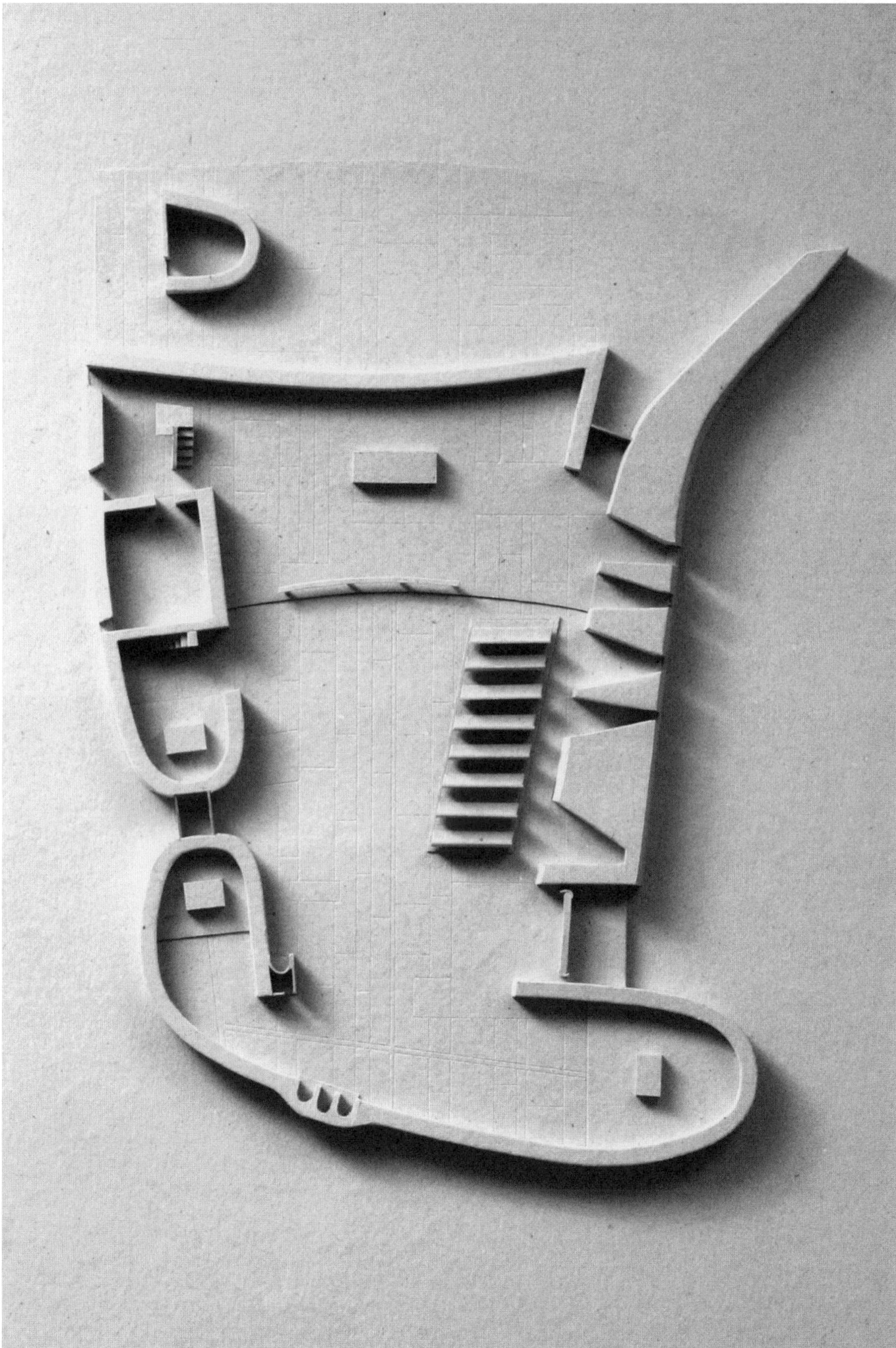

[46]

[47]
Like a three-dimensional section on a drawing, the building model reveals itself to the viewer.
[48]
Roof structures can be all that is required to display the construction principle.
[49]
Reduced to their structural components, complex buildings can be depicted simply.

questions based on sound, comprehensible information.

Among all the building model types, the landscape architect's preferred medium is the garden model. Landscape architects also use the model as a working tool to depict the (garden) landscape architectural aspects of their design. The architecture of the building plays a secondary role in these models, where the design of the surrounding environment is much more important. External works are often displayed in combination with the building, but here they are the focus of the model.

4. Interior models – scales 1:50, 1:20, 1:10

Not every construction project is concerned with the design of a complete building. It is often the case that planning and design apply only to a relatively small area of space. Interior models are also used to represent a part of a complex building that the architect would like to investigate as representative of the whole building, i.e., a module or a repeated element. Examples of this include (model) residential units in an apartment complex or the hotel room, which are represented in detail to serve as an example and explain the concept of a whole hotel complex. This model type is extremely useful for representing spaces used for religious purposes, where particular emphasis is placed on the fitting out and room-defining elements being in accord with the way light is directed within the space. This model can also be used for sequences of prominent spaces, such as circulation routes with staircases, building entrances, which act as interfaces between the indoors and outdoors, or generally speaking all spaces that must have a particularly high-quality spatial character.

[48]

[49]

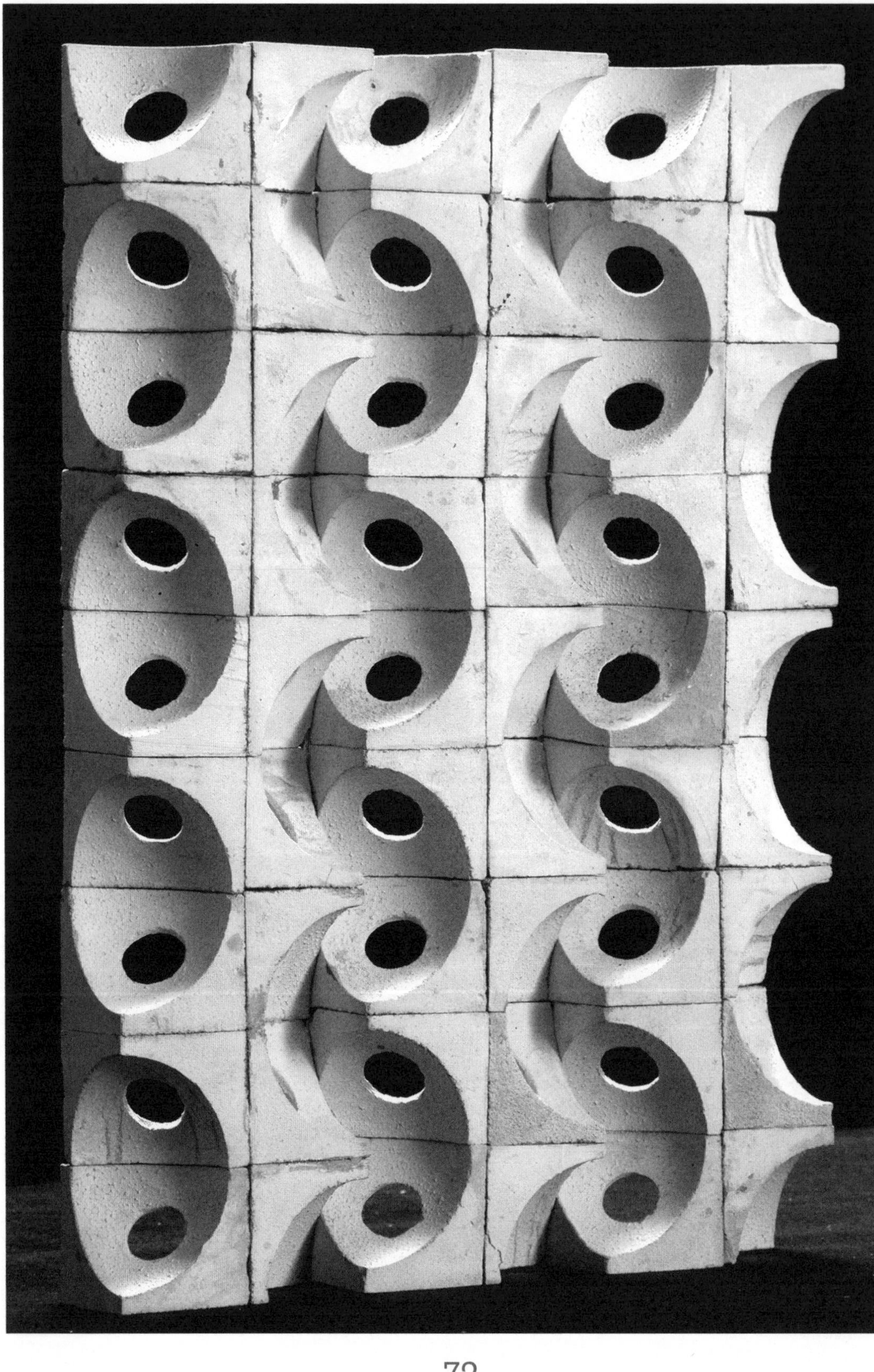

[50]

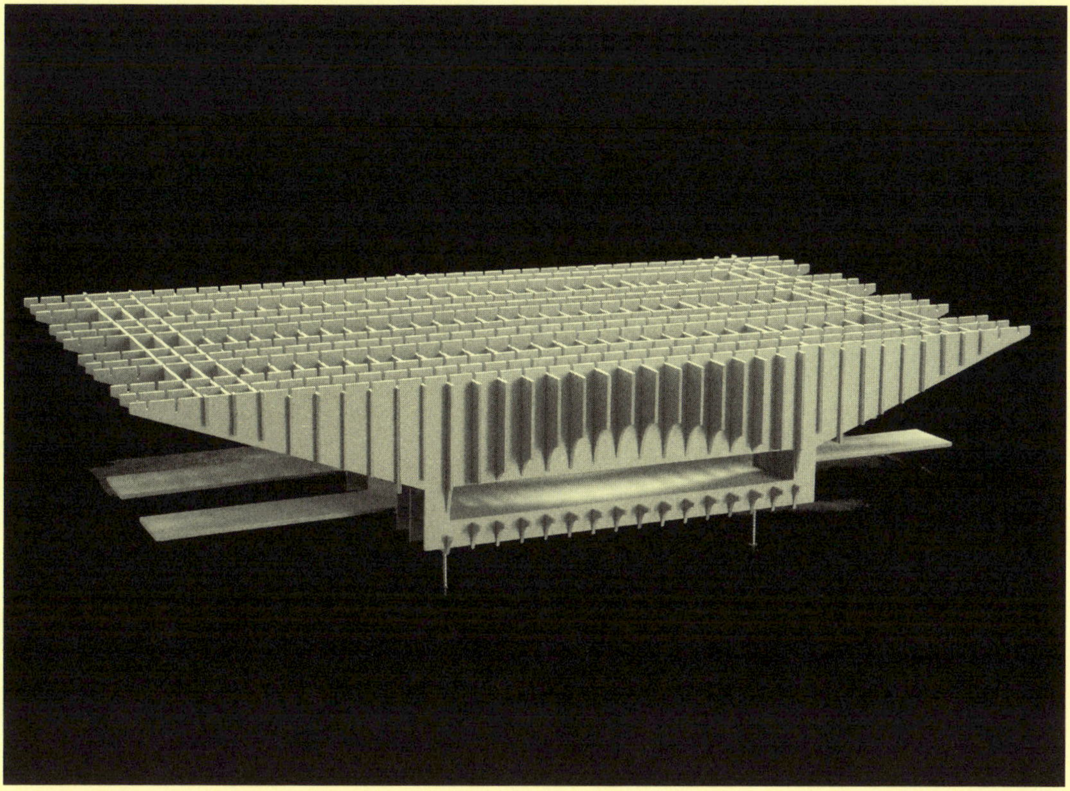

[51]

[52]

[53]

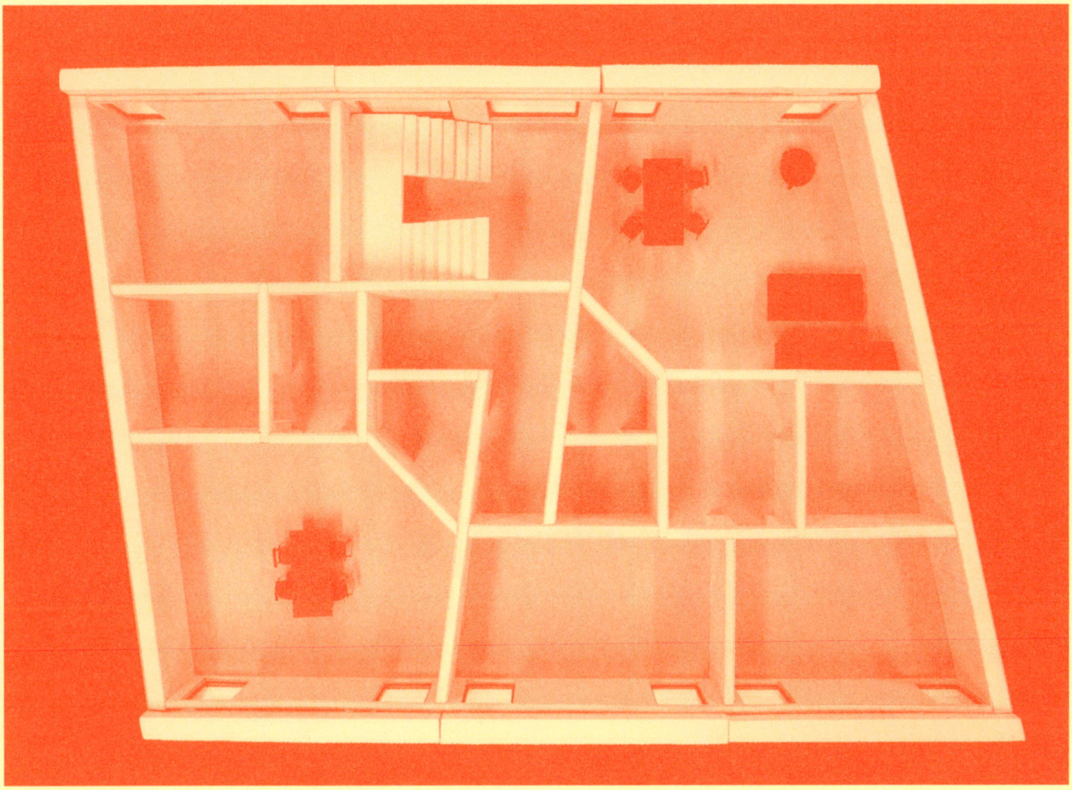

[54]

Interior architects can also work more realistically at these scales, because the detailed representation of parts such as doors, windows, and room-defining surfaces influences the later character of the space. In a similar way, the impression of the designer's concept can be further enhanced by the use of additional fittings and movable furniture such as chairs and tables. It is immediately apparent that this description also fits the type of model popularly known as a doll's house. Obviously, model makers and architects would like to differentiate their work from these models. As mentioned before, reduction to just a few materials and the intention of precisely implementing the architectural idea play a significant role in ensuring the model does not become kitsch or romantic but remains abstract in character in every case.

However, the model could be used the other way around to explore the concept and determine which materials work with the interior model design theme and, during the design process, to try out different materials for the floor, wall, and ceiling.

Another aspect not to be overlooked is the effect of natural light in the space, which is important in all model types. Large interior models can also simulate lighting situations using artificial light.

[50]
The structure of the architectural object is represented in the final material, i.e., concrete.

[51]
Reduced to the load-bearing components, the partial model shows the structure in three dimensions.

[52]
For historic timber structures, the structural model made the principles of the carpentry legible. 1:50, plywood and wooden strips

[53]
The colors employed in depicting the contents push the garden into the foreground ahead of the architectural elements.

[54]
The eye is drawn by the color and detailing in this representation of the garden design.

[55]
The focus on a single floor level is like a drawing with a "built" third dimension. Floor plan model of an apartment. 1:20

[55]

[56]

[56]
Small design projects such as micro apartments often call for this specific form of representation, which may include furniture in the model. 1:20
[57]
The interior model shows the exterior as an abstract box and presents the thermalized interior space when the facade is opened. 1:20
[58]
The materials in the model simulate the character of the design. 1:20

facade design because it determines the appearance of the building to the outside world. The demand for detail in the design at this stage is very high; the material for the facade has either been specified beforehand or can be displayed in the model for discussion. This type of model can help settle practical questions, such as how the openings are designed, whether a window element is flush with the inside or outside of the plane of the facade, or how a lintel or windowsill should appear from the inside and the outside. In a similar way to the previously described interior model, facade models can be abstract or true to the original in the choice of material, depending on which aspects of the model are to be addressed.

5. Facade models – scales 1:50, 1:20, 1:10

Taking representation in the model to the next level, the focus no longer lies on the building as a whole but is limited to certain specific individual components, in this case the facade.

The facade is the external envelope or skin. Architects often spend a great deal of time on the

6. Detail models – scales 1:20, 1:10, 1:5, 1:2, 1:1

The experimental character of detail models may be sufficient motivation to leave the plane of the drawing and enter the field of model making. How do the parts articulate and fit together physically in the practical sense? The thought process of design is transferred into the model, sometimes by building

[57]

[58]

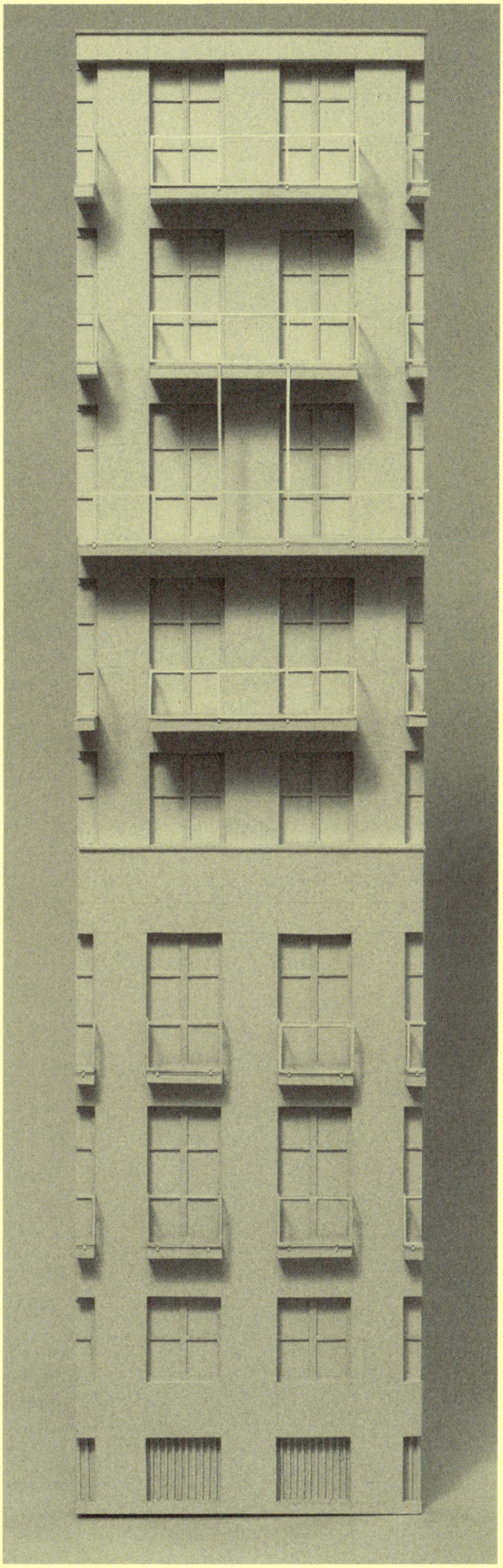

[59]

[09]

[61]

[62]

[62]

88

Typology

up layers of construction to simulate this later activity or investigate how the various constructional cross sections will fit together. Corner solutions are often modeled like this, as are all the transitions between components. How does the building plinth handle the transition from the ground to the wall? How can a corner be incorporated into the wall and how is this detail treated at the top end of the structure, at the roof? And if all this experimentation proves a success, the model is not simply set to one side; it is used again later to communicate the knowledge gained to those who have to build it in reality. Any areas not properly addressed in a detailed design may well stand out much later on site. The model is an excellent way of simulating specific and – most usefully – unusual, and therefore largely unfamiliar, processes that the architect is expecting to see play out later on the building site. In contrast to the building model, where the level of abstraction means that most of the dimensional details of fitting the construction together are solved by the application of glue, the detail model is required to develop and define the detailed aspects of these rules. By the way it is put together, every connection, every geometric junction point, every inserted or screwed connection has an influence on the detail and therefore the whole architecture. The detail model is not only useful as an end result, it also reveals valuable knowledge of how items join together and relate to one another as the model is being made.

[59]
Representation of a historical facade, 1:20, gray paperboard

[60]
Facade models in the form of strips in a single material through which all the architectural design elements are expressed. 1:20, gray paperboard

[61]
The architectural principle of a relief facade is shown in abstract with this representation of the pure plastic surface, without other details. 1:50, two-dimensional plaster model

[62]
The architect Egon Eiermann developed and tested the effect of light and the concrete honeycombs' geometry on the facade of the Kaiser Wilhelm Memorial Church in Berlin using models.

[63]
Cutaway model of the facade and the rooms behind it, 1:20, gray paperboard

[64]
A piece of the design is simulated at a scale of 1:1 using the originally intended materials.

In addition to the simulation of important details in the context of the architecture, furniture models can be made to scales of 1:10 to 1:1. They can be either used as staffage in the interior models described above to examine the dimensional relationships of items, or investigated as designed pieces of furniture in themselves. Here the detail model is shown to be one of the most effective among all other model types in realizing the eventual prototype.

7. Mock-up – scale 1:1

As the scale approaches that of the built environment, the question arises as to where the transition takes place between the architectural model and the completed architecture.

Of course, the term "model" is to a certain extent imprecise, because it can have several meanings and extend beyond the topic of architecture to find application elsewhere. Perhaps the only point of general agreement is that a model is an image of reality and that this image is a simplification. Not all features and attributes of reality that are capable of being depicted will find themselves in the model. What is modeled is a selection of certain aspects that relate to the model.

From these considerations, the full-scale models that the architect builds, or more often has someone build, can be described as architectural models, because they often take on an experimental character precisely in order to enable a final decision to be made about the construction of building components such as facades with their highly elemental structure. This can only be done using the actual material and of course to the actual size. The section modeled naturally gives a very real impression of the final appearance.

Mock-ups in modern times are often made to investigate curtain wall facades in a panel on one of the stories of the building, usually on site during the construction of the building or as an exhibit to be

[65]

[65]
Miniature versions of furniture can be displayed as a design element and examined in the architectural context in the furniture model.

[66]
Architects from Meixner Schlüter Wendt developed and checked the design of Dornbusch Church, Frankfurt am Main, using a model built to a scale of 1:1.

displayed to the public close to the site boundary fence. This particular form of model is often adopted for structures that will have a particularly high-profile presence in a public space. A commissioned trial panel is often made for clients to show them how the building will later look. The model in this case is not only the model. It also assumes the significance of a sample.

At many times in the history of architecture, people have seen fit to go to the expense and trouble of creating a model of a complete component of the building or even the whole building in simpler alternative materials. The Building Academy in Berlin designed by Karl Friedrich Schinkel, for instance, was fashioned to its original external dimensions using scaffolding, which was then covered with fabric on which the facade was printed to create the impression from a distance of the original presence of the building in the urban space, in order to win the public's support for the reconstruction of the building.

8. The completed building – scale 1:1

At the end of a series of model types, can the realized design also be considered a type of model? Is a building also an architectural model to a scale of 1:1? If every model is merely an anticipation of reality, does the realized building represent this reality or does it still possess the character of a model? To clients, the building is certainly not a model in the sense of the definition, but to architects the interpretation of their work is still open.

[66]

[67]

Models communicate a multilayered expression of architecture: the surrounding context, the program and the typology are "narrated" just as much as the character lent to the architectural space by materiality and the way light is directed.

Function

4

Why do people make models? The reasons for making a model must be understood very precisely if it is to achieve its objective. Without an answer to that question, any attempt to justify the role of the architectural model in design is bound to fail. How will the model be used? How justifiable is the cost? Today there are many and varied ways of representation and proven methods of arriving at a final design. Can an apparently traditional method such as making models really still be the right way of designing architectural space?

If, for example, private clients who have their own houses designed by architects were asked whether they had the design communicated to them using a 1:50 scale model, the answer would be no. Models are expensive, models incur costs, and therefore they are understandably not the most common means of communicating such information here. Although it is obvious that the model would be a tremendous help to the lay client in following and completely understanding the work of the architect, the designer shies away from the cost for the above reasons.

[68]

[68]
Dominikus Böhm, Christkönigkirche, Mainz, 1925, Mainz, model 1:50, MDF
[69]
Dominikus Böhm, Garnisonkirche (Sankt Johann Baptist), side chapel, Neu-Ulm, 1922–26, Neu-Ulm, model 1:20, MDF

95

Function

[70]

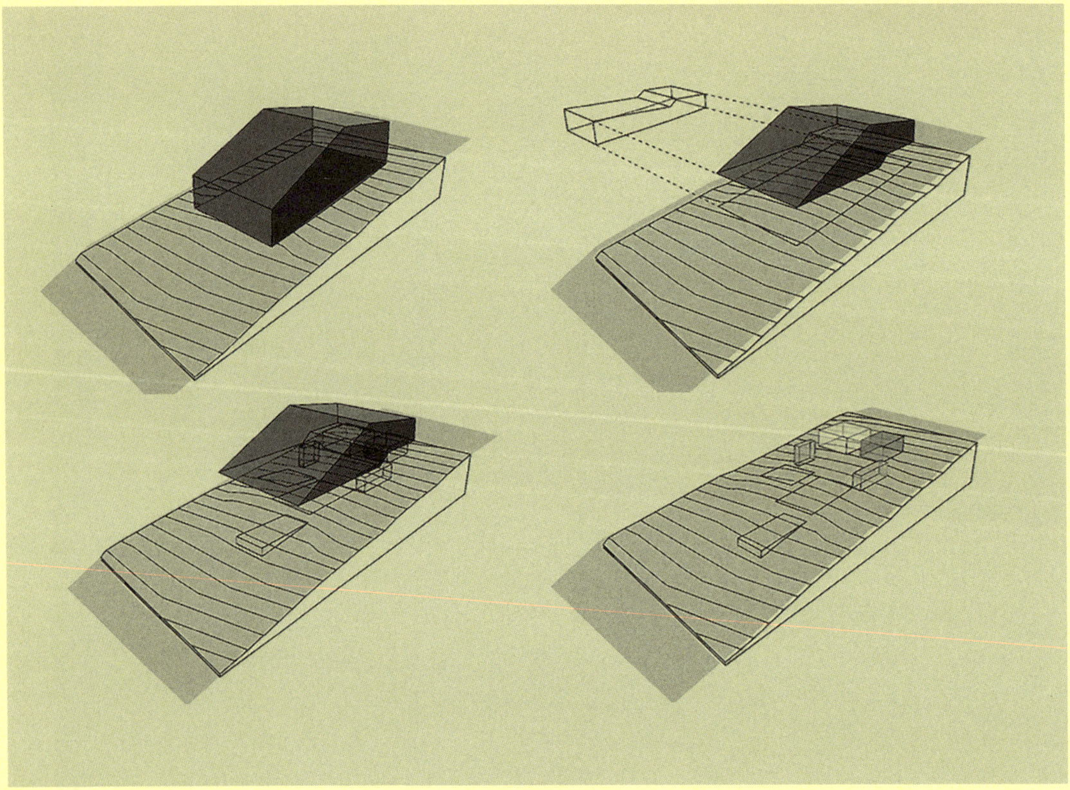

[71]

[72]

[73]

[74]

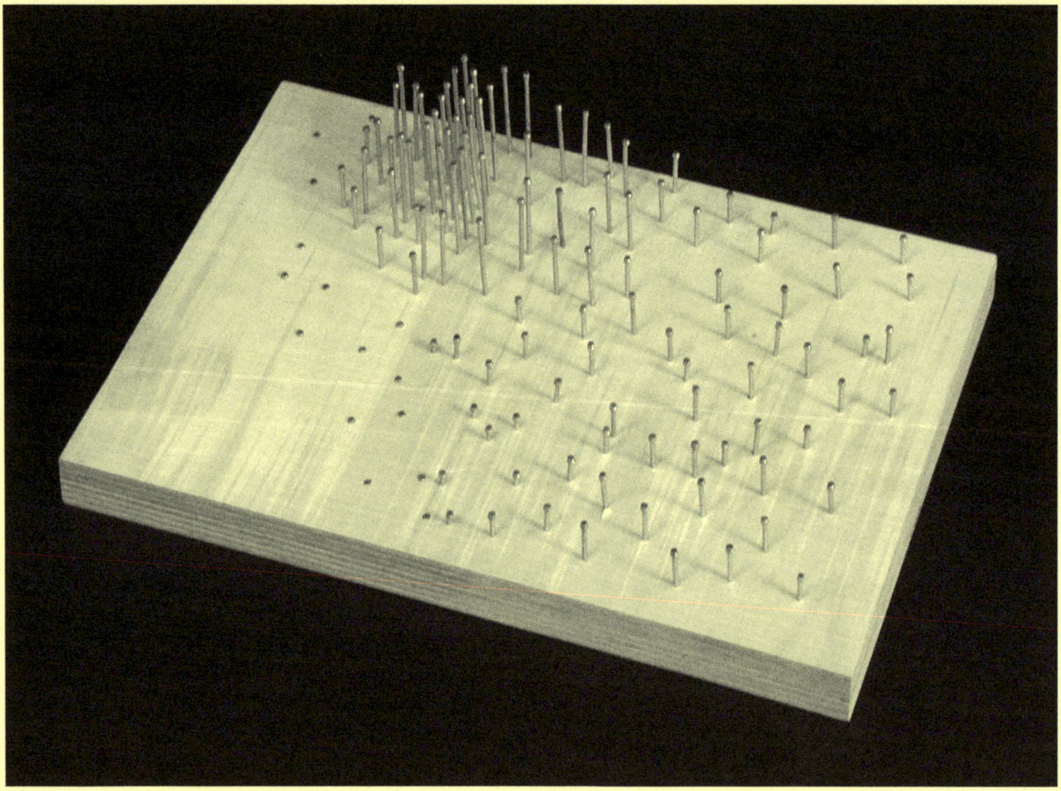

[75]

[70]
The freehand sketch communicates the spatial idea, the fundamental principles of the design. Meixner Schlüter Wendt Architekten, Haus F, 2005-07
[71]
The pictogram explains graphically and represents three dimensionally the thoughts of the architect about the architectural design. Meixner Schlüter Wendt Architekten, Haus F, 2005-07
[72]
The architectural model is the tangible medium by which the design is captured and assessed against all its architectural and spatial criteria. Meixner Schlüter Wendt Architekten, Haus F, 2005-07
[73]
The completed house is the result at the end of the design process. The architecture was developed using a combination of all methods. Meixner Schlüter Wendt Architekten, Haus F, 2005-07
[74]
Used experimentally, abstract models provide impetus for the formulation of the architectural idea – operating at an artistic level.
[75]
The analysis of the place and its specific conditions – relevant to the design – together with the sketches can be translated into an abstract model as a study. Here nails make clear the density and physical heights of the layout of a city or topography.

With all other basic forms of representation – the sketch, drawing, or the image produced on a computer – it is interesting to note that the question of justifying their existence does not arise immediately. The model has always been present as a medium, but it is not an ever-present stage in design. Perhaps not every commission requires a model to ensure its success either, given that professional skill guarantees that the designed space does not rely on a miniature building in order to be verified and the communication of the design idea to others can be done through alternative media. The people who can only profit from the interaction of all means of representation, however, are those who are not versed in the interpretation of drawings, and they are without exception pleased to have the project explained by means of a model. Who in this situation would still prefer to look at the drawings pinned to the presentation board?

The function of the architectural model during design

In addition to content, designing is above all a chronological process. An idea reaches maturity over the period of time made available to it and continuously receives new impetus by interaction with the design as it progresses. Not infrequently the model, if one is wanted or required, is not made until after the final version of the design has been determined. All decisions have been made, all possible versions and alternatives examined and weighed against each other and, so to speak, after the editorial deadline has passed – with the completion of the drawings and perspective views – comes the model. Not necessarily from some inner motivation, but rather more because the architectural competition documents or the brief for the design project completed as part of coursework includes the requirement to make one.

Throughout the whole design process, model making can be used alongside the usual tools of representation to develop and visualize architecture. The advantage of the model is obvious. The model works in three dimensions and that makes it unique from the beginning.

How can the model be used in the various design phases? In what ways is the architectural model significant in these phases? The function of the model changes during the course of the design. At the beginning, there is the experiment, i.e., examination and three-dimensional verification of the sketched design approaches. In the subsequent

[77]

Function

[77]

[78]

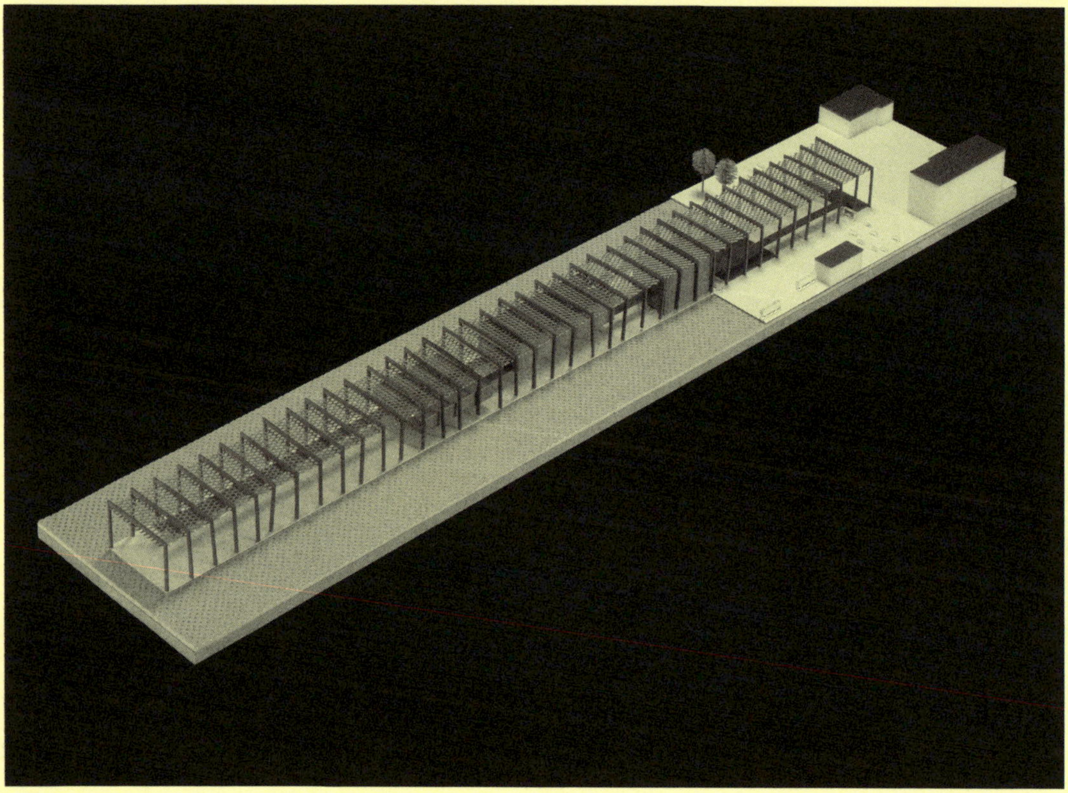

[79]

[76]
As a material that can be kneaded, plasticine is ideal for coming up with concepts using means that are almost playful.
[77]
With their high degree of abstraction, concept models communicate the formal and architectural thoughts at the heart of the real architectural design.
[78]
The search for form and the sculptural approach on the architectural level is achieved using clay models.
[79]
The building model stands in contrast to a three-dimensional collage, which depicts the conceptual content in an abstract manner.
[80]
Many study models used to discover concepts and forms allow decisions about the later design process to be made on a spatial level.

working up of the design, its representation and communication through the model moves into the spotlight.

1. Concept models – the idea in model form – no real scale

How does one do design? The design starts with an analysis of the location and architectural task, initially made perceivable with a model of the surroundings. The designer looks for the idea, expresses it as a sketch on paper and, in the best case, this solution-finding process results in conceptual models. The idea is made tangible and can be examined for the first time. This could be as a realistically shaped, kneaded plasticine volume in an urban space model to allow the viewer an immediate understanding of the effect of the proposed building on and its relationship with the pre-existing situation. Or the designer develops the idea by taking a metaphorical approach, with the model being seen as an abstract study that supplies nothing more than a metaphor transformed into a sculptural object as an attempt to explain the idea.

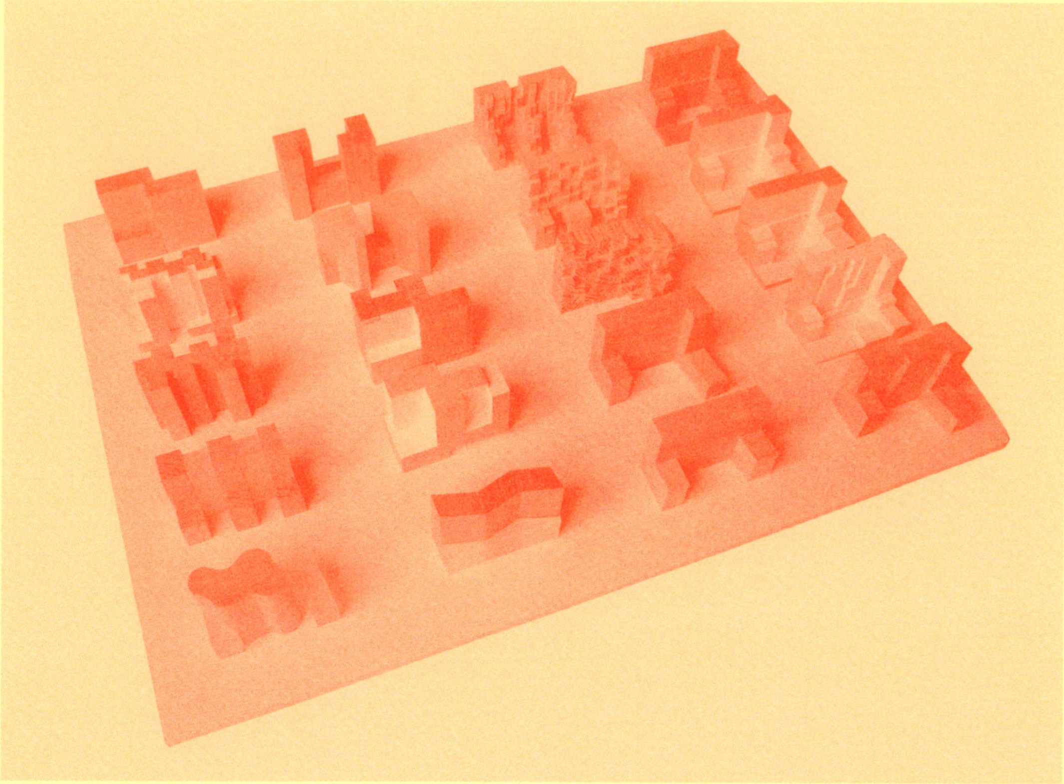
[80]

[81]

[82]

[81]
Working models are easily recognized because they look unfinished, temporary, and improvised.

[82]
A traditional type of working model is the polystyrene model, which can be cut to shape with a hot-wire cutter and assembled very quickly.

[83]
Working models are concerned neither with perfection nor finality but rather with rendering the spatial idea comprehensible in as simple and purposeful way as possible.

As the concept is pushed further and developed, thinking and designing with the model takes place in the same way it does in sketches and drawings. As a consequence, the concept model can be thought of as the equivalent of the first sketches, pictograms, and attempts to generate ideas that occur at the start of the project. The conceptual approach develops from the analysis of the location and the design parameters. Simple abstract models can help to examine these approaches experimentally or to visualize and communicate them. It is often effective to use materials, colors, and shapes to develop, examine and communicate the first important results of the design in a bold and simple way.

At this stage, the model is easy to change and quick to form or reform, which makes the dynamics of changing and further developing the design almost like a game. It is not intended to show the virtues of a finished object, but rather to concentrate on the imprecision in the expression and the still fluid boundary conditions of the design. The model can be used to study the design by employing simple manual techniques preferably without the need for mechanical tools.

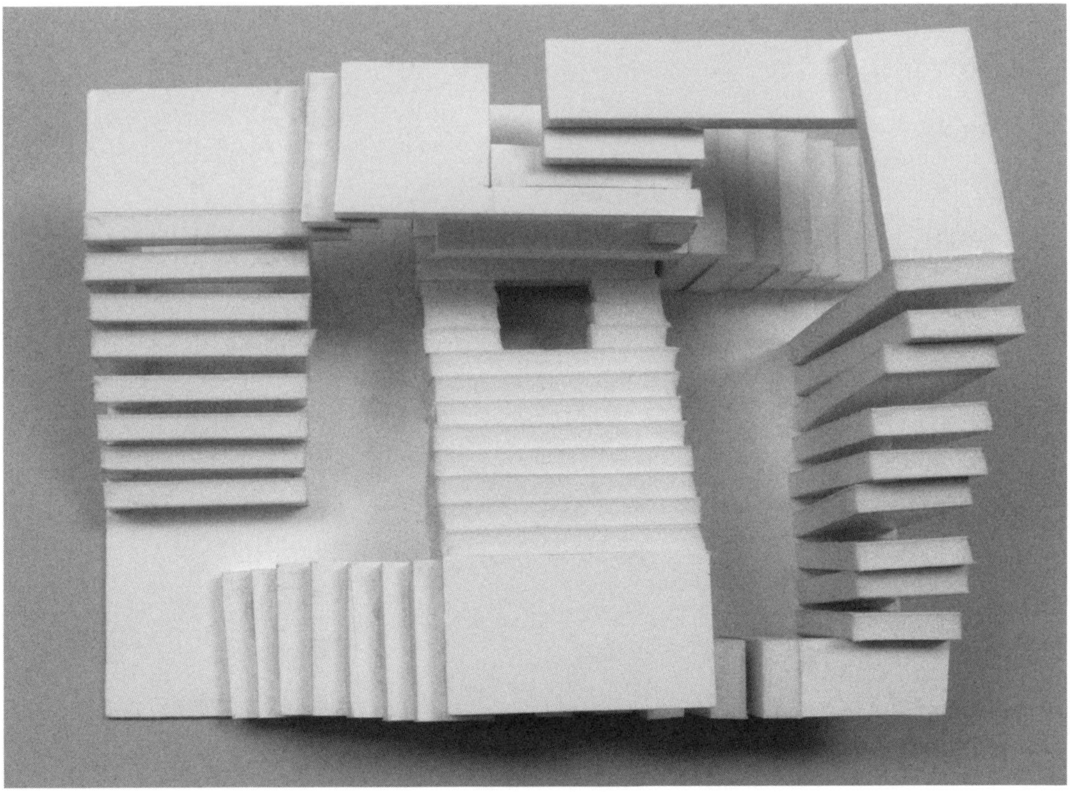

[83]

[84]

[85]

2. Working models – three-dimensional sketches – at a scale adequate for the model type

Working models have that name because designers do in fact work with them. They are unfinished, indeed they are constantly corrected, modified, or changed. Here as well, the designer is still working methodically in the area of three-dimensional sketches, which are articulated in the working model. Design thoughts are examined with the objective of quickly assessing whether these thoughts also have traction as three-dimensional objects. Besides helping to examine the designer's thoughts, the model can also be used to develop them and push them further. Sometimes it starts with building something, without knowing what it could lead to in the end – like a pencil stroke on a sketch. In other words, the end of the stroke is not predictable at the start; it is spontaneously created.

Here it is still not about precision or any claim to perfection, but much more about making the quality of the idea recognizable and exposing the errors – a piece of cardboard or paperboard recently glued in place can be quickly torn off again following such a discovery. Many students of architecture look back painfully at this moment, when lecturers verbally tear apart the carefully and lovingly assembled model to point out its defects.

It is therefore helpful to use materials that are easy to work with and can be joined simply with readily available tools. This allows the model to be built and rebuilt repeatedly until the solution is found or effortlessly discarded if it is still incapable of delivering the anticipated spatial result. Working models are indispensable companions in the complete design. Whether it is at the level of urban design or the architectural formulation of the design up to the detailing, working models supply crucial information and stimulation.

[84]
With working models, everything is permissible in order to transfer the expression to three dimensions, even plasticine or simple corrugated cardboard, which are less durable.

[85]
These kinds of formable materials are perfect for lending the model an almost sculptural and plastic character that expresses the design's own dynamic.

3. Presentation models – ideational and mature – at a scale adequate for the model type

The presentation model for the design brings together all the previously worked-up content to create a clear expression of the design. At this late stage the choice of materials and processes used for the creation of the model can no longer be made casually, because the viewer perceives the expression not only from the content but also from the esthetics and the craftsmanship, which simply should not be underestimated in facilitating this perception. The presentation model must also take into account architectural aspects and differentiates itself clearly from the experimental character of its predecessors. Of course, it still represents a temporary state, because the model may be used for an architectural competition or for an exhibition of the design at the client's premises. The model still does not represent the final design that will be used in the construction of the building, but the degree of accuracy should still be relatively high.

In every case, the presentation model should be regarded as the equivalent of presentation drawings. Both means of representation complement one another in the type and quality of their depiction and give the design its own identity.

Presentation models in architecture courses

Even during their studies, many architects come to be highly motivated to construct models with care and passion to complete their coursework

110

Function

and final degree projects. Their aim is to develop their own design and end a project with models that have been completed as perfectly as possible. Interestingly, one phenomenon is always observed in the end phases of this work, namely, there is never enough time to implement the students' intended high standards for the quality of the model by the deadline. A phenomenon that is repeated in professional practice, at least for the end phases of preparation for architectural competitions. Time pressure at the end appears to be the best motor to bring a design to a close and the model often represents, in terms of progress, the stage of the design on the last night before the submission. The mandatory model plays a role in the final critiques at university or when awarding prizes at architectural competitions, if not the deciding role at times, in promoting the design or in communicating the design in all its qualitative aspects. Why is the model not created first and the drawings completed at the end? Since design is a process that may not even be completed on site, the design can profit to the maximum extent only if the model is created before the drawing and therefore can also supply momentum and feedback for the design process. For this reason, the drawings should follow on from the model. Even the final model still has the potential of a working model and is available to analyze and discover more about the design.

The cost and effort involved in presentation models are great, not least because of the choice of materials, i.e., durable, high-grade materials such as fine-grained woods, strong and rigid materials that allow for the model to be used over longer periods and its original condition preserved. Paper and card are very suitable for working models, but do not have the necessary durability and light-resistance. Therefore they are recommended only in certain circumstances for presentation purposes. In addition – a point of view that is not to be overlooked – every model claims time that could be spent on other work. No one is suggesting the figurative orgy-of-materials approach, but the sensible and purposeful use of materials is not insignificant to the success of the model. Reference to the reality of the model's appearance and the final construction must be made here because the decision about the materials for the actual building is also simulated in making the model.

With the decision about the materials, it is also clear that the higher cost associated with machines and tools would have to be accommodated and that the model maker may no longer have the option of working independently with simple tools, but will have to rely on model making workshops with their professional equipment. This is when logistical and deadline issues suddenly come to the fore in the question of scheduling when the presentation model is to be made. At this stage, the process bears a striking resemblance to the actual construction, albeit a situation which is very much more manageable by comparison.

[86]
Working models have a property denied to presentation models, i.e., by leaving out many details and content, they focus on the core expression. Walls, ceilings, and openings formulate the space.

Presentation models in practice – final construction models

The presentation model has a further important task in the architectural office, that is, the model may be used during construction. The content of the model is for the most part decided and real at this stage in anticipation of what will soon be built at a scale of 1:1 on the construction site. This model, as the first material implementation of the design, takes on even more importance for it may remain the only material manifestation, should the client decide not to go ahead with its construction. As a final construction model, its functions may be extended to include the spatial conception and the associated architectural order, which are the established themes that the model communicates. However, the aspects of economic efficiency, which the proposed concept of the architect addresses, in conjunction with the load-bearing structure and material construction of the building at a suitable scale become a constituent part of the consideration and can be made into a theme in the model. Basically, the model will help in convincing the decision makers that the design is ready for construction. Models of buildings at a scale of 1:1 attain this air of completeness and provide convincing evidence that the design should be implemented. Any

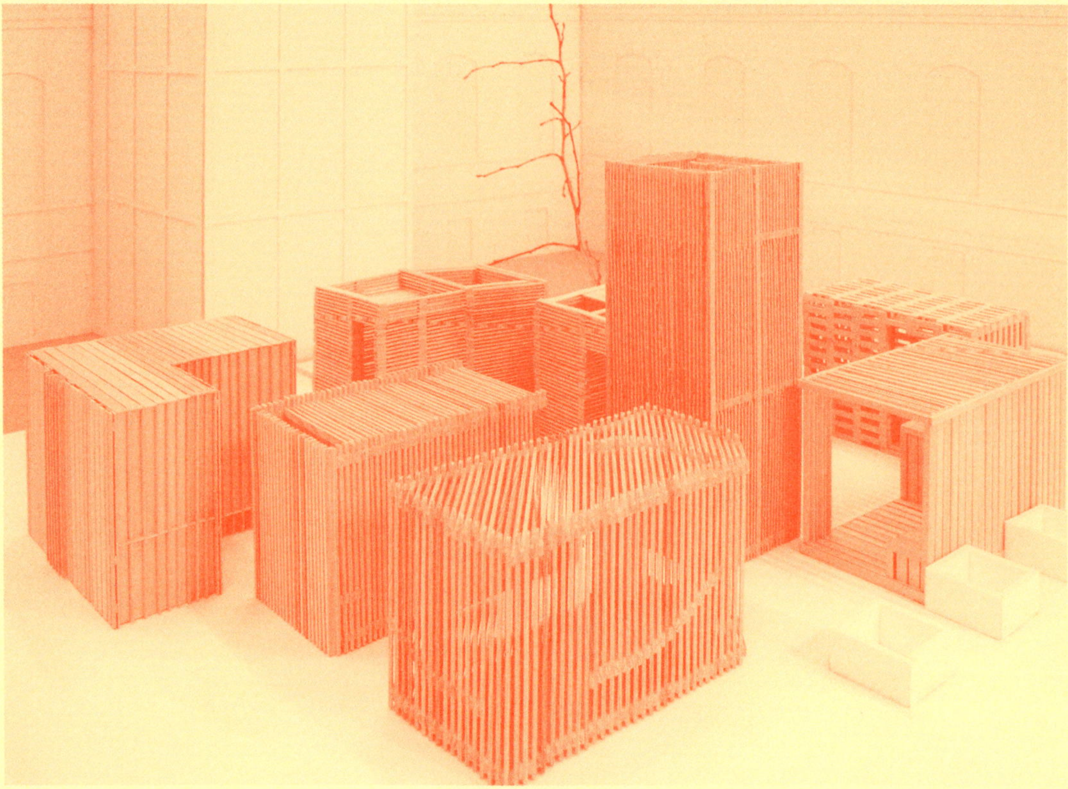

[89]

[90]

[87]
The high-quality material gives the presentation model a touch of class and communicates the seriousness of the design idea to the viewer. Monochrome wooden model with wood veneer and strips
[88]
With much love for detail and handicraft skills, the model displays a host of information contained in the design. Polychromatic model with paperboard, wood veneers, and printed paper
[89]
Presentation model of temporary pavilions as a three-dimensional installation at a scale of 1:20, wood pulp board and wooden rods
[90]
Modeling the pavilions as a three-dimensional installation at a scale of 1:1, by means of the realization and leap in scale up to reality, the building still retains its model-like character. Wooden boards, joined with screws

questions affecting the character and the anticipated quality of the building that are still unresolved or not apparent at this stage can be answered at the end only by the completed building. The model has served its purpose. The model assumes the function of all the tools available to the designer in the verification and depiction but in a much more convincing way, because representation on the computer monitor lacks the third dimension necessary to appear truly spatial. The scope of use of models in the architectural office depends on how complex the representation is in the model, in other words, the larger the scale, the greater the truth of the detail and the effect of the space. All the information in the drawings, every design decision, may and should flow into making the model to ensure that the model is as close as possible to reality. Above all with scales of the order of 1:20, the model maker ought to consider precisely how the character and specific properties of the materials proposed for the real building can be transferred into the model in order to influence the result. In the best circumstances, the same material proposed for the real building should be used for the model. The model can also explain very well how the transition between the building and the external space works. The sections on the drawings – on sloping ground – always give information in point format showing how the building is inserted into the organically shaped topography. The model, on the other hand, integrates all the points shown on the cross sections.

Model and reality

The architectural model depicts the real object at a reduced scale. This does not work without the trick of omitting unimportant aspects of the built reality by abstraction. There is also considerable difference between the reality that the model communicates by suggestion and which each viewer will perceive subjectively, and the possible built reality. Models mislead their viewers and this is their intention. To what extent does the final building, which the model represents in miniature and stands in for, measure up to this impression? The model is still free from the constraints and demands that the real construction presents to the architect.

Moreover, as with sketches and drawings, the model, in its expression, takes on a personal aspect from its authorship, which can be read like the handwriting style of a writer. This makes every model one of a kind and, like the finished building, it is normally not repeatable in the entire process of its creation. A model is unique, as is every completed building.

[91]
Miniaturization of the architecture requires precise craftsmanship.

Model Construction Site

5

How do you build a good model? What makes a good model and what criteria can be used to judge it?

Being engaged with the process of making models is an extremely diverse and thoroughly fascinating experience. For young students, this could be their first contact with the building process and it is certainly not unreasonable to liken constructing a model to constructing a building. For a simple working model in corrugated cardboard and film or plastic wrap, the insights into the processes are not as extensive as they would be for a larger model in which the material is more demanding in terms of its application and handling.

Theory has it that for the architect, the experience of building models is also the experience of realizing the design, even if it is in miniature. Not a small number of architectural designs are utopian in their approach. The model provides utopia with the stage on which it can at least become comprehensible, that is, the model brings the design out of the plane of the drawing.

[92]

The following steps set out the process of model making – with continual references to the real construction of a building. As with all tips and advice, these steps should be seen as ideas on how it could be done. It hardly needs saying that the diversity of the available options when making models, the manifold possibilities and processes, does not lag far behind that of real life. An actual construction plan (or assembly instructions) that is to be followed step-by-step, something like cooking by following a recipe out of a cookbook, does not exist for model making. Plans and instructions are often included with kits for making model aircraft, ships, and railways, but not for architectural models, which is why the processes are clearly and distinctly different.

The approach is much more one of thinking about what is possible. What is the current state of the technology and model making insofar as it can be assessed? This chapter seeks to provide an overview of the craftsmanship, techniques and processes involved in creating small architectures.

From concept to model

Before building can start, there has to be a process of design. This analogy with architecture is apparent from the very beginning. The model has a similar need for a design, which can be considered as the interpretation of the architectural design at the level of the model. The model maker takes information in abstract form from the architectural design then thinks about how this can be transformed down to the required scale. In terms of practicality, there must be plans or drawings. What should be built? The building depicted on the drawing is broken down in the model design into the individual components relevant to model construction, viz., volumes, areas, and rods (straight lines). Out of this emerges the model's design concept, which should result in an architectural model that convincingly represents the building esthetics and scope, and shows a high level of craftsmanship. The analysis can begin with the following considerations and questions:

[92]
The model confronts some of the fundamental questions of design: the proportions and composition of the parts with respect to one another, in this case the relationship between the mounting board (plinth) and the modeled object.

- Intention of the model
- Who is its target
- Which architectural aspects should be physically expressed
- Scope of the model
- Material
- Color/colorfulness
- Scale and the actual physical size of the model
- Level of abstraction (coarse or detailed depiction)
- Type of model
- Composition
- Proportion(s)
- Cost effectiveness of the model

It is wise to consider the architectural model and its construction as a project in its own right. Planning and execution are a composite part of the process of manufacture. A model is a mini-project and therefore its costs must be managed. An expensive model is not necessarily a good model. As a student and later as a professional, everyone develops their own specific approach to model making – in the same way as they develop a handwriting style.

Design – the principles of composition and proportion

Perhaps it feels like the repetition of an idea, déjà-vu on the way to realizing a project, i.e., the basic questions of design theory keep coming up. Without these considerations of architectural design, the model will not work and cannot be built. This involves an analysis of the requirements of the miniature, in particular, at what level of abstraction the design should be transferred from the drawing into the model. These considerations begin, for example, with the mounting board and its size, square or golden ratio or the exact geometric shape of the plot. How should materials be combined with one another (a dialog between opposites using contrast to communicate the message)? These questions are best approached experimentally and explored in small trials and work samples to see which composition of materials offers the most satisfactory design solution. On site, the contractor submits samples of materials for the architect to make the final selection.

This choice in each case is made in the context of the overall effect. As in architecture, the elements comprising the model should go together to form a single unit. This is how composition and proportion are used in art and especially in architecture. Transferred to the context of architectural modeling, how these aspects of design theory also affect the model is summarized below:

- How much of the surroundings should be included and what should the position of the building be in this frame of reference to best communicate the three-dimensional message in the sense of the urban context?
- What should be the size of the designed object in relation to the size of the overall representation?
- Should the designed object be in the center of the model or is there a compelling spatial argument not to do this?
- An edge position in the urban context would be translated similarly into an edge position in the model.
- Would contrasting pairs best express the model, opaque or transparent, coarse or fine detail, realistic or abstract, monochrome or color?

In considering how a model can be abstract yet interpret the actual design, the modeler finds out intuitively in the main how the model can be designed to best effect. Many design decisions about the model are self-evident or have already played a role in the architectural design. Everything centers on the question of what image the architect has in mind for the design and how to make this image visible to everyone else.

Material – the substances from which models are made

Again, like the real world, the question is always what sort of material should be used for the model? The diversity of choice is probably less than for building the real object, but the crucial specialist skills for model making and the model maker's own creativity in the sense of using materials in different ways offer sufficient possibilities for how to materialize the model.

Working models are usually built from materials that are more than adequate for conveying the experimental character of the object. Paper and cardboard are ideal because they are inexpensive to buy and easy to work with. Other principles apply to a presentation model – as outlined earlier, its construction has to satisfy higher requirements. The focus is on obtaining the optimum result.

Usually the important criteria include the choice of material, the scale of representation, what tools and machines are available, and the craftsmanship skills and talents the model maker has to provide. Model making is an art learned through practice. Hardly any model maker starts as an expert; each model is a vehicle for learning.

As soon as the decision has been made about whether a model is to be built from paperboard, wood, metal, or plastic, the next question arises, i.e., should a monochrome model be created completely in any one of these materials on an abstract level of representation? Basically, all the components can be made in any of these traditional materials, which is precisely the appeal of model making. Monochrome models abstract all parts based on their presence in context and reduce them to create the abstract form and expression. Facades, for example,

[93]
Through the choice of material (colored plaster), the model achieves an integrated form and legibility at all scales. Likewise, the material communicates an expressive massiveness, while the type of processing communicates the level of abstraction in terms of vagueness and approximation, which allows the viewer adequate scope for the imagination.

[94]
Competition model in the form of a hybrid of an urban design and a building model. Through the abstraction the few details give only an impression of the architectural idea. 1:500, polystyrene, painted white

[95]
Wooden models are traditional because of the strongly expressive naturalness of the material and underline the value of the model as an object. 1:50, wooden rods, coated

[96]
Models made from plastics such as polystyrene and acrylic glass allow higher precision and communicate the accuracy of modern steel-glass structures in the miniature; the materiality remains in the background. 1:50

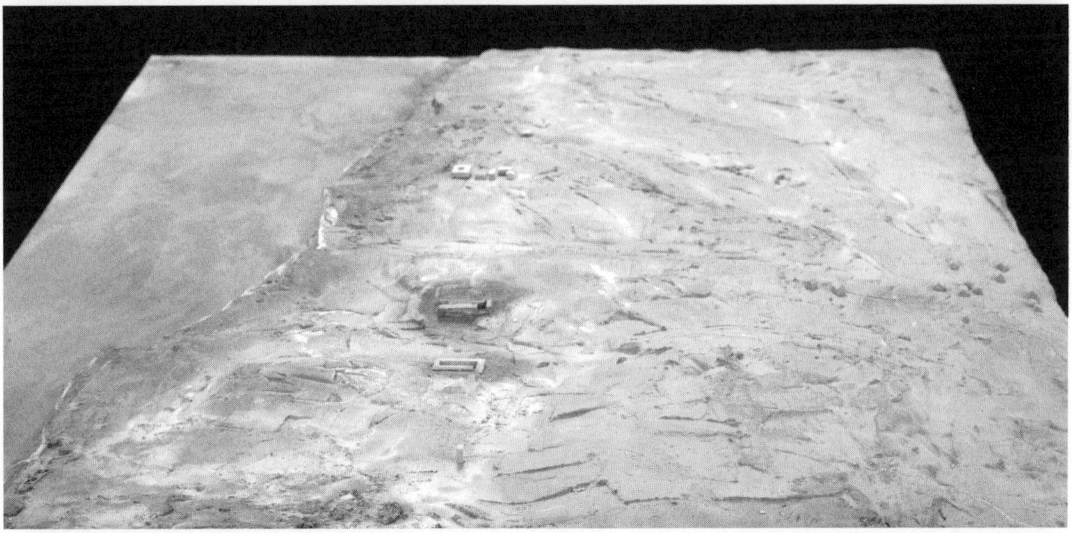

[93]

Model Construction Site

[94]

[95]

[96]

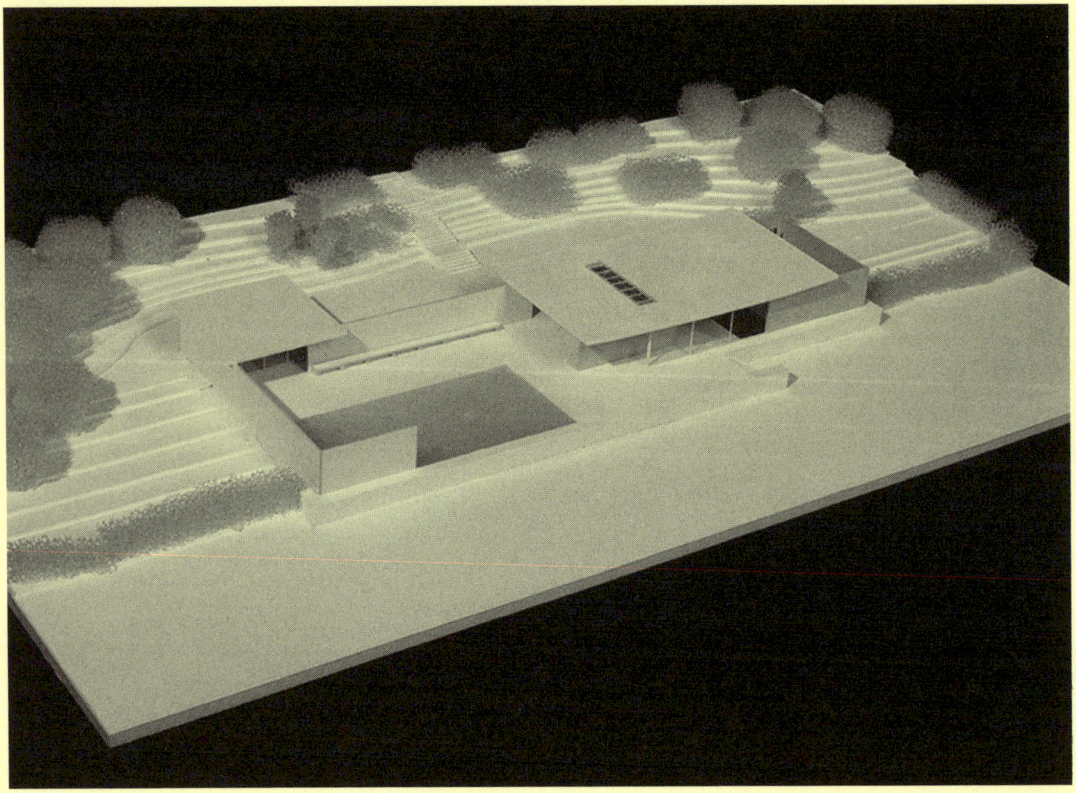

[97]

[97]
Ludwig Mies van der Rohe, Barcelona Pavilion, 1929. Conceptual model in two versions, one in wood and the other in paperboard, 1:50, plywood and white paperboard respectively. The choice of material for making the model has an effect on the final result, irrespective of the architectural design, and that effect is evident here.

become reliefs because transparent parts such as windows are either not shown or shown as dummy panels. One material is sufficient if it has the potential to be worked and used in a variety of ways and have its surfaces differentiated using tools or applying coatings (paint or varnish), if this is what is wanted. Models made of paperboard, above all gray paperboard, but also those made of polystyrene and plaster that have been coated with matte white paint represent the best-known examples of monochrome models. In expressing an architectural idea, these models, through the unity of their color and surface properties, offer an advantage, i.e., the material retreats from the focus of perception in favor of the abstract space.

A monochrome model is frequently selected for architectural competitions. These are usually to a scale of 1:500 and constitute a mixture of urban design and building model, and are reduced to the most significant aspects of the design.

In addition to models made out of paperboard or polystyrene, there are those that are fashioned from a single type of wood and they, too, achieve this reduction. The attraction of these timber models is that the special characteristics of the wood lend a vitality to the model, despite the uniformity of the material. The nuances of its grain and natural color emphasize the uniqueness of the model. Moreover, just as old wooden objects in museums and archives age very well and develop a patina, these effects do not mar the esthetics of the model, indeed just the opposite.

In addition to monochrome models like these, many more are made with several materials, with the model maker's material concept translating the differentiation within the model in terms of different materials. The mounting board with the surrounding land consists of a material that is also used to model existing buildings, with only the new building catching the eye of the beholder through the use of its own, different material. As in reality, the designer uses a mixture of materials in the model to express the various architectural elements.

Design in the architecture	Design in the architectural model
Transparent and translucent components: Glazed building envelope with rodlike load-bearing structure with the focus on transparency	**Model components:** Transparent films such as PVC or acrylic glass, or the glass is left out and only the load-bearing structure is shown
Massive components: Masonry, natural stone, or fair-faced concrete	**Model components:** Solid wood or, if the scale is suitable, the same material
Structural frames: Timber frames and steel skeletal structures (lightweight and filigree latticework structures)	**Model components:** Filigree constructions in wooden or polystyrene profiles of suitable cross section
Facade: Combination of smooth, fine-textured plaster areas *with* coarse, horizontally textured brickwork *or* unfinished natural stone surfaces	**Model facade:** Combination of smooth paperboard, wood veneer, or MDF *with* joints cut into the surface with a blade *or* surfaces roughened with sandpaper or removal of the smooth outer layer in the case of paperboard or MDF

[98]

[99]

[100]

In principle, the contrasting elements that the architect fashions into the theme of his architectural idea can also be adapted directly into the concept of the model. Why not? The idea can be implemented in the model in a still more focused way and exaggerated to an extent. Abstraction in the sense of reduction to one material using this approach would not be the right way, because the clarity and conciseness of the idea would not be communicated to the appropriate extent.

At this point, however, reference must be made to a phenomenon that occurs in architecture and in model making, that is, the use of many materials is often too much! The famous principle of Ludwig Mies van der Rohe also holds true in architectural model making, "Less is more!" Otherwise the result can be overpowering. In the negative sense, this can be described as an orgy of materials, which impairs rather than delivers the legibility and expressiveness of the model. The architect's creative drive should also be expressed in the model.

Abstraction or love of detail?

The type of representation and the consequent processing of the selected materials are other important criteria for the quality of the model. All model makers follow a similar path of development, as per the earlier reference to a handwriting style or, in the context of model, the question of how they go about making the model.

The question that is continually perplexing model makers is how to handle abstraction. The model maker may seek to take into account, even at the smallest scale, the precise detail of the design in the representation, because of a conviction that this would enrich the model. On the other hand, the preference may be for a model that is very reduced and limited in expression. Therefore, the final choice is for a simple implementation, which enlivens the model because of what is left out. Whichever path is chosen, it is important to be consistent and adopt the same degree of abstraction throughout. It makes little sense, for example, to reproduce the building's surroundings precisely and with a great deal of fine detail if the implanted architectural design lacks this love of detail.

Each scale predetermines in a real sense the level of abstraction for the model maker. A window at a scale of 1:500 will either not be shown or, in our age of digital cutting tools, be cut out perhaps as a rectangular opening in the workpiece. At a scale of 1:100, this window will be much clearer. It has a role to play, showing whether it has a frame, is subdivided and how it sits in the window reveal. At scales of 1:50 and 1:20, it appears even more real. There may be frames, casements and, if appropriate, perhaps even glazing.

The level of abstraction in the model is directly related to the drawings and such interactions in the type of representation are helpful. The level of abstraction of a door element on the drawing largely determines its level of abstraction on the model. Abstraction is always linked with the question of the essence of the architectural design. The model maker should decide all this or at least think it over again before picking up the modeling knife.

As with drawings, abstraction gives rise to a free space which viewers have at their disposal and in which they can exercise their imagination. The scope for imagination is naturally wider if the model is more abstract and less realistic. The model has an effect on the viewers, who are influenced by every decision on how each part is represented. The modeler can and should direct perception in a positive sense. A detailed model, perfectly designed and constructed to create the right impression, causes the user to believe that the architectural design is equally well thought out and differentiated. The model is therefore the ideal medium at this point in time to achieve these aims. The strategy is recommended above all for providing people who require an idea of the finished building with a final basis for

[98]
The window as an abstract opening in the surface at a scale of 1:500 or 1:200.
[99]
The window with a frame that contains all the important architectural elements is shown at a scale of 1:100 or 1:50.
[100]
The window with all the components such as casement, glass, and mullion, detailed to represent reality at a scale of 1:20 or 1:10.

making decisions on how the architectural design should be implemented. For a client about to make a large investment, it would seem perfectly justifiable to present something as close to reality as possible. In the case of experimental studies, however, a better tactic would be to express the architectural design with some lack of focus.

There are rarely any limits to the love of detail. Even to the professional model maker, the degree of precision to which digital machines can work is amazing; a laser-cut paperboard model is precise to a fraction of a millimeter, which would never be possible to achieve with a manual tool nor is it perceivable to the naked eye. The representation of detail can go right up to the limits of what is technically feasible. A good rule of thumb says that the point where any more detailed representation would not be worthwhile is the point where manual methods would not produce a more precise result. When it is no longer possible to cut out a window opening neatly at the selected scale, then it is obviously smaller than the width of the blade and there is no need to display it.

Perfection is a fetish

Although it cannot be emphasized often enough that model making in architecture is distinctly different to the hobby of building models of aircraft, ships, or railways, one feature is shared by all model makers, i.e., the tendency towards perfectionism! This applies to everyone who approaches the task with passion and may even have chosen architectural modeling as their career. The exact working of materials and the use of fine motor skills is common to all people who make models. Like watchmakers, they have the reputation of working with a magnifying glass and tweezers and valuing precision above all. Using instruments that function at accuracies of fractions of a millimeter, they check their work as they go along, always aware how important dimensional accuracy is for the end result. At a scale of 1:200, the model maker can see straight away if a column in a row of columns deviates by a few millimeters from the vertical. A closer look at this scale will readily reveal any lack of neatness. Up to a certain extent, the model appeals to viewers because it is a handmade article and is therefore distinctive and gives off a sense of liveliness. It is no different for the actual building. When did you ever hear a craftsman say something is beautiful? Nothing built is ever perfect! This is always the case when you construct something. Therefore, it is only justifiable in some circumstances to demand this level of perfection when making a presentation model. Perfection alone does not make a good model nor can it guarantee one. Not a small number of students go to their tutors with a roughly crafted working model and are greeted with enthusiasm. Improvisation in a model can communicate ideas, without the need for a great deal of work and expense and yet depict the design in a clear, legible manner. More important than the trend towards technically perfect results is the model maker's handwriting style referred to earlier, which can be read from the model and can lend its power of expression to the object. A rough level of craftsmanship and representation can even be considered just as much a strategic design medium as the perfectly built model, depending on the form of reality the model is meant to convey.

Materials and modeling resources

Without materials there can be no model. These are the ingredients needed to materialize the idea. Only with the material can the model maker accomplish that leap into physically tangible reality. Choosing a suitable material is part of the model maker's art. Just as in practice, it becomes clear how many different materials there are and how all of them are suitable for building! Every material is special, not only with respect to its properties, how it can be worked and the specific impression it creates, but also in terms of the costs involved in using it.

Selecting a suitable material

The level of abstraction of the model generally has a big influence on the choice of model making material, in terms of its properties and the resulting expression. What in reality is rough or smooth, shiny or matte, delicate or massive and heavy must also be articulated in the model. Whether the model maker uses traditional model making materials such as paperboard and wood or adapts other materials in an unusual and imaginative way plays no role. What matters is that the user engages intensively with the effect and selects the model material precisely based on the aspect of suitability. Glass is transparent and effective; these properties are also shared by transparent plastic film. Horizontal layers of masonry are typical of brick; narrow strips of paperboard or wood interpret this in the model. Water surfaces identify themselves by reflecting light and the edges of the banks that surround them; a reflective plastic sheet precisely communicates this effect. Using a greater thickness or a darker material as backing suggests the depth below the surface.

The type of model, the chosen scale, the time, and the budget inevitably help in decisions about the material concept. Many architects go on to develop their own taste for certain materials and become practiced in handling them. There is an abundance of materials suitable for architectural models. The material science properties of the model maker's most important materials are described below.

Paper, paperboard and cardboard

These materials are so popular because of the many ways they can be used. They are the model maker's first choice for anything from simple working models right up to final presentation models because

Summarizing the most important materials from the point of view of their origin, properties and processing options.

Material	Format / type	Processing
Paper / paperboard / cardboard	Sheets from DIN A4 to lengths over 1.0 m	Cutting / folding / gluing / coating
Wood / wood-based material	Block, board, veneer, rods, and profiles	Sawing / filing / sanding / gluing / polishing / coating / waxing / oiling
Metals	Sheets, foil, tubes, rods, and profiles	Sawing / soldering / welding / gluing / grit blasting / polishing /coating
Plastics	Blocks, sheets, films, rods, and profiles	Cutting / sawing / sanding / coating / painting
Plaster / concrete	Single substance or mixtures (powder), made liquid with water	Building formwork / casting / curing / abrading / coating / coloring
Wax / soap	Solid at room temperature, made liquid by heating	Heating / casting / cooling / coloring
Clay / modeling clay / plasticine / formable materials	Block, deformable	Molding / kneading / drying / firing / abrading / coating
Composite materials	Glued-laminated boards, dimensionally stable and flat	
Other materials, not specifically intended for model making	Various	

Paper, paperboard, and cardboard

Type	Properties	Use	Processing
Drawing paper / card	• Brilliant white color • Weight per unit area 120 – 900 g/m² • Smooth or textured surface	• For white surfaces or small-scale building models	• Easy to cut • Very good to glue • Surface can be given a colored coating
Colored paper	• Wide choice of colors • Weight per unit area 130 g/m² • Smooth surface	• For all kinds of colored models (concepts, collages)	• Easy to cut • Very good to glue
Photographic card	• Wide choice of colors • Weight per unit area 300 g/m² • Smooth surface	• For all kinds of colored models (concepts, collages)	• Easy to cut • Very good to glue
Gray paperboard	• Warm gray color • Made from recycled paper • Thicknesses: 0.6 – 2.5 mm • Smooth or rough surface	• Universal use for all types of models	• Easy to cut • Very good to glue • Surface can be given a colored coating
Wood pulp board (Finnboard)	• Beige color similar to light-colored wood • Thicknesses: 1.0 – 4.0 mm • Smooth surface "Soft" • Yellows under UV light	• Universal use for all types of models • The light-colored surface is suitable for simulating daylight sequences	• Easy to cut • Very good to glue • Surface can be given a colored coating
Screen printing card	• White color • Wood pulp board coated both sides with smooth paper, cut edges beige • Thicknesses: 1.0 – 3.0 mm	• Mainly used for (white) interior models • The light-colored surface is suitable for simulating all kinds of daylight sequences	• Easy to cut • Very good to glue • Surface can be given a colored coating
Corrugated cardboard	• Light-brown color • One or both sides smooth • Covering a corrugated internal structure • Strong in the longitudinal direction of the corrugations, deformable transversely • Thicknesses: 1.5 – 6.0 mm • Available with one or two corrugated layers	• Mainly suitable for working models, topology contour models	• Easy to cut • Very good to glue • Surface can be given a colored coating
Honeycomb board	• Light-brown color • Covered with smooth surface both sides • Very dimensionally stable and lightweight • Thicknesses: 5.0 – 50.0 mm	• For mounting boards or large interior models	• Easy to cut and saw! • Very good to glue • Surface can be given a colored coating

[101]

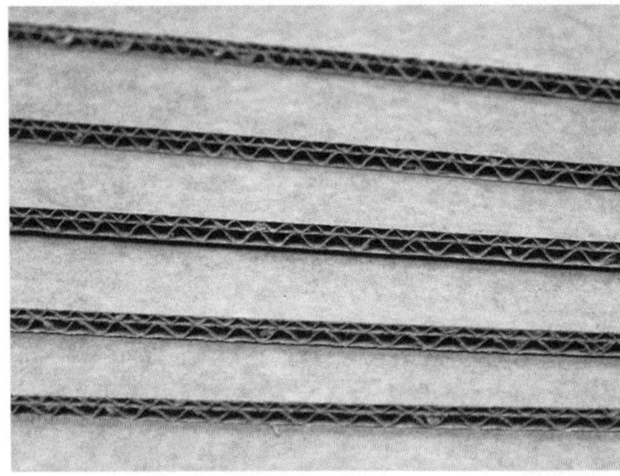

[103]

[102]

[104]

[101]
The blocks for massing models are usually of the following woods: balsa, maple, and linden.
[102]
Rods (profiles) in the following woods are used to represent slender components: mahogany, walnut, pear, pine, and balsa.
[103]
Corrugated cardboard – smooth on the surface, corrugated in section
[104]
Other typical model making woods, used mainly as veneer board: abachi, pear, linden, and mahogany.
[105]
Oak – a beige-yellow-grained wood
[106]
Cherry – a reddish-grained wood
[107]
Teak – a brown-grained wood
[108]
Wenge – a dark-brown fine-grained wood
[109]
Zebrawood – a brown heavily grained wood
[110]
Birch – a light-colored "patterned" wood
[111]
Maple – a light-colored fine-grained wood
[112]
Beech – a slightly red fine-grained wood

[105]

[106]

[107]

[108]

[109]

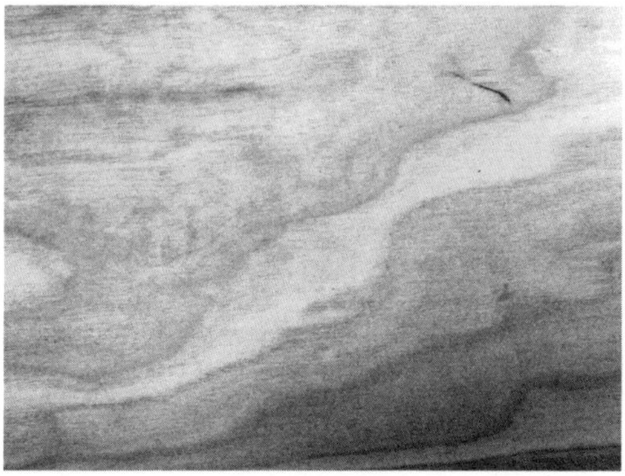

[110]

[111]

[112]

they are inexpensive, versatile, very easy to work with, and do not require the use of machines. Moreover, paperboard is available in a wide range of forms. There is bound to be one to suit every representation situation.

Wood and wood-based materials

Many descriptions of architectural models do not stem from the model type, but rather from the material used to build them. Wooden models have been with us since the Renaissance. The model of the dome of St. Peter's Basilica by Michelangelo was made out of linden (also known as the lime tree). Much more time-consuming to work with than any paperboard, wood lasts far longer and communicates retention of value and stability – not unimportant criteria for the architectural design it seeks to represent. Solid wood – a natural and renewable raw material – exerts a claim to legitimacy far better than any other material for presentation models, because it appeals to the viewer's emotions.

The two categories – natural wood and wood-based materials – are related to one another in terms of working techniques and properties but must be considered separately. In the central European region alone there are over 1500 different usable types of wood. Which wood is therefore suitable for the model? For small format models and pieces, it is advantageous to use light-colored wood that has a fine, plain natural grain and is free of knots.

Wood-based materials

Genus	Property	Use	Processing
Chipboard	• Reasonably priced wood board made from waste wood chips • Rough surface • Thicknesses: 6.0 – 22.0 mm	• For mounting boards • For depicting rough and textured surfaces in combination with surface treatment	• Processed like wood • Very good to glue • Can warp if exposed to excessive moisture
MDF (Medium density fiberboard)	• Hard, high-density wood fiberboard with homogeneous, smooth surface texture • High dimensional stability with flat surface • Natural brown color or stained	• For mounting boards, raised-relief models and complete, large-scale building models	• Processed like wood • Very good to glue • The surface can be treated, e.g. with clear varnish or a stain
Plywood (Birch, beech, poplar)	• Glued-laminated wood boards made of several layers of these wood types • Visible grain and color depends on the wood used	• For raised-relief and building models • Used as an alternative to solid wood in models because plywood is strong even in thin sections	• Easy to process with a utility knife or saw, in some cases with a router (birch)
Coreboard	• Plywood made of glued wood • Visible grain and same color as that of the wood used	• For mounting boards and bases	• Processed like wood

Woods

Genus	Property	Use	Processing
Abachi	• Hardwood • Soft and light • Low strength • Straw-yellow color • Slightly linear grain	• Veneer to represent wooden surfaces (smooth, grooved, textured)	• Easy to cut with a utility knife (in the direction of the fibers) • Very good to glue • Spray adhesive can be applied over full surface
Maple	• Hardwood • Soft • Yellowish natural white color • Finely differentiated grain	• Can be used for all model types • Wooden blocks for urban planning models • Veneers for surfaces and models of buildings	• With standard wood-processing tools • Sawing and sanding • Very good to glue
Balsa	• Tropical wood • Extremely light and soft • Slightly shiny and light surface, velvety • Homogeneous texture	• Veneer to represent wooden surfaces • Wood profiles to represent buildings	• Easy to cut with utility knife or saw • The wood breaks easily along the grain • Very good to glue
Pear	• Hardwood • Evenly textured • Light reddish brown color with an elegant surface • Homogeneous texture	• Can be used for all model types • Wooden blocks for urban planning models • Veneers for surfaces and models of buildings	• With standard wood-processing tools • Sawing and sanding • Very good to glue
Beech	• Hardwood • Strong with uniform fiber structure • Light brown-reddish color • Homogeneous texture with oints	• Can be used for all model types • Wooden blocks for urban planning models • Veneers for surfaces and models of buildings	• With standard wood-processing tools • Sawing and sanding • Very good to glue
Pine	• Softwood • Strong and linear fiber structure • Yellow color • Striking linear grain (vivid)	• Wood profiles for structural and construction models using the strength of the wood	• Depending on the dimensions, pine is very easy to cut with a utility knife or saw
Linden	• Hardwood • Short-fibred and soft • Yellowish, light color • Homogeneous texture	• One of the most commonly used woods in model making • It is suitable for almost all purposes	• Depending on the dimensions, linden is very easy to cut with a utility knife or saw
Mahogany	• Tropical wood • Very hard • Slightly shiny surface • Dark, reddish-brown color • Linear, fine grain	• Used to contrast with all light-colored woods or model making materials	• Due to its hardness, it can be processed only with a saw or sanding tools
Walnut	• Hardwood • Hard • Depending on its origin: fine or coarse grain • Deep, dark-brown color	• Used to contrast with all light-colored woods or model making materials • Elegant appearance	• With standard wood-processing tools • Sawing and sanding • Very good to glue

[113]
Metal profiles are used for representing filigree constructions: brass, stainless steel, aluminum.
[114]
Shiny metal sheets
[115]
Perforated aluminum sheet
[116]
Perforated steel sheet

Metals

Metals have two characteristics that make them a popular choice. It is possible to make extremely thin and filigree components and the presence of metal in the context with other surfaces can reinforce the expressiveness of the model. Often model makers use a particular metal because this metal is the one that will be used in the actual building. In these cases, substitution by other materials is hardly possible. Only a metal creates an effect like a metal.

[113]

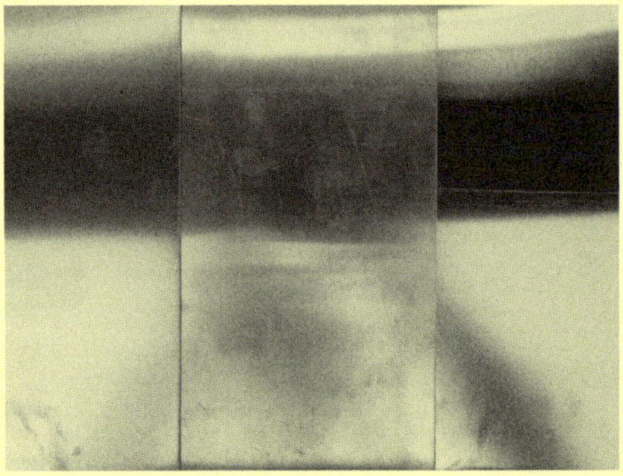
[114]

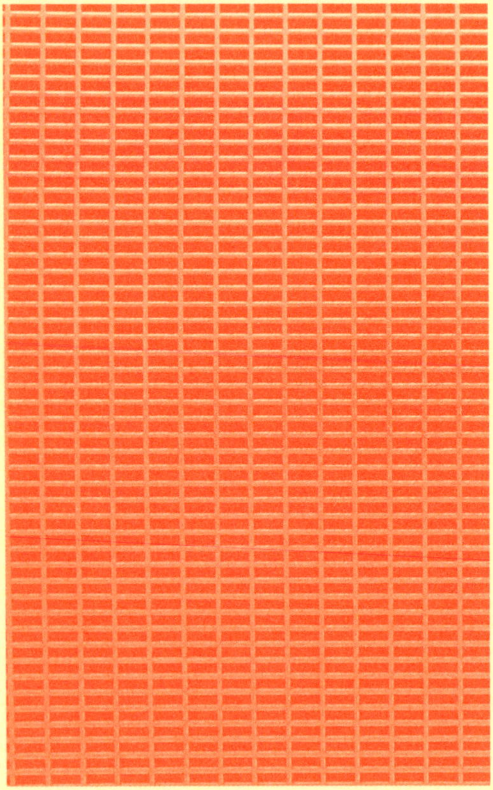
[115]

[116]

Metals

Metal	Property	Use	Processing
Aluminum	• Silver-white color • Resistant to water and atmospheric oxygen due to a dense oxide layer • Non-magnetic	• Film, sheet, perforated sheets, and profiles • Representation of metallic components e.g. corrugated sheet for the roof	• Cannot be soldered • Glued connections (universal adhesive) • Cut with tin snips or metal-cutting saws
Iron/steel	• Dark silvery color • Corrodes in contact with moisture and oxygen to form reddish-brown rust • Magnetic	• Sheets, perforated sheets, rods, and profiles • Representation of metal components • Profiles can be used for structural models (beams and columns).	• Can be soldered and welded or glued with universal adhesive • Use corrosion-resistant (e.g. zinc-plated) materials or apply coating or paint • Cut with tin snips or metal-cutting saws
Stainless steel	• Silver-gray color • Smooth, fine texture • Passivating layer prevents rusting • Non-magnetic	• Sheet and profiles • Can be used in areas exposed to moisture (e.g. external areas)	• Glued connections (universal adhesive) • Cut with tin snips or metal-cutting saws
Copper	• The only red metal, oxidizes in contact with air, turning red first, then green	• Sheet and profiles • Used in the model to represent copper	• Can be soldered or easily glued • Can be processed with metal tools, depending on the thickness
Brass	• Alloy of copper and zinc • Red to light red, depending on copper content. A golden color can be produced with higher proportions of zinc	• Sheet and profiles • Used to represent shiny (golden) surfaces • Profiles can be used for structural models (beams and columns)	• Can be soldered or easily glued • Can be processed with metal tools, depending on the thickness

Plastics

A number of different plastics are used in model making. They are used mainly where high precision and accurate detail – close to perfection – is required. Plastics are also inexpensive, strong, and lightweight. Polystyrene (PS) and acrylic glass (Plexiglas) are the most frequently used types.

Plastics

Plastic	Property	Use	Processing
Polystyrene (PS)	• Impact resistant and hard • Matte white surface • Not UV resistant • Thicknesses: 0.3–5.0 mm	• Universal use in all areas of model making	• Easy to cut with utility knives • Surface excellent for sanding • Can be machined and glued together • Easy to varnish or paint
Polystyrene rigid foam	• Extruded polystyrene rigid foam • Dense, rigid foam • Block material in various thicknesses and colors	• Perfect for buildings and volumes, especially for urban planning models	• Cuts precisely with hot-wire cutter • Can be glued only with suitable adhesives (otherwise it dissolves, "eaten away")
Polypropylene (PP)	• Heat resistant, tough and tear-resistant plastic • Transparent or opaque film • Scratch-resistant surface • UV resistant • Thicknesses: 0.5–1.2 mm	• As a translucent film, it is excellent for representing matte glass surfaces or for internally illuminated objects	• Easy to cut with utility knives • Can be bent sharply, folded, grooved, notched, embossed or stamped in all sorts of ways • Almost impossible to glue!
Polyvinyl chloride (PVC)	• Can be transparent or opaque, depending on the type of manufacture • Various material thicknesses	• Transparent films are suitable for representing glass in the model, thin film can be used for many other purposes	• Easy to cut with utility knives • It can be drilled, routed or turned • PVC surfaces can be glued together with ordinary plastic glue or contact adhesives
Polycarbonate (PC)	• High-strength, impact-resistant plastic • Weather resistant • Fine surface texture • Transparent or milky films	• Transparent films are suitable for representing glass in the model. Thin films can be used for many purposes	• Easy to cut with utility knives • Thicker sheets can be scored and broken off • PC surfaces can be glued with solvent or contact adhesive
Acrylic glass (PMMA)	• "Plexiglass" • High transparency and brilliance, very good optical properties, similar to glass • Weather-resistant plastic • Available in transparent milky or opaque form	• As a transparent material for representing glass or water	• Thin foils can be easily cut with a utility knife • Thicker material must be broken off or sawn • Easily glued with solvents, contact adhesives or special glues for acrylic glass

Modeling and castable materials

Architecture is often represented from an artistic – almost sculptural – point of view in the model. As soon as this physical expression becomes the focus of our perception, thoughts again turn to materials and their suitability for model making – nothing is better for expressing the art within an architectural design.

One material in particular has a very long tradition of doing this and challenges wood as the oldest model making material: plaster. People have regularly produced miniature replicas or copies of ornamental architectural artwork in plaster. Models made entirely out of plaster in one cast are seldom seen today. This is not least because of how these models are manufactured. To cast something in plaster requires a precise negative mold. In architectural design competitions, the basic model of the plot with the existing buildings is still made in this way. A negative mold means the model can be reproduced many times, which is the great advantage of this method. To reduce the physical weight of the plaster object, the inside is made hollow or from a lightweight filling, for example, clay, wire mesh or rigid foam. Like models made completely out of wood, plaster models form their own category within architectural models.

Soap (glycerin) and wax are two further examples of castable materials used for model making. Both are made liquid by heating, are poured into molds, and harden again in the air. Soap – milky transparent in its solid form – can be used to great atmospheric effect to represent water.

The method of making models out of the same material as the actual building was mentioned earlier. One such material, fair-faced concrete, is much beloved by architects. Fair-faced concrete – with the mix modified to take account of the scale of the model in the fineness of the aggregates – is handled and processed exactly as it is on the actual construction site, i.e., build the formwork, oil the surfaces, and then

[117]
Plaster: landscape model, 1:1 000

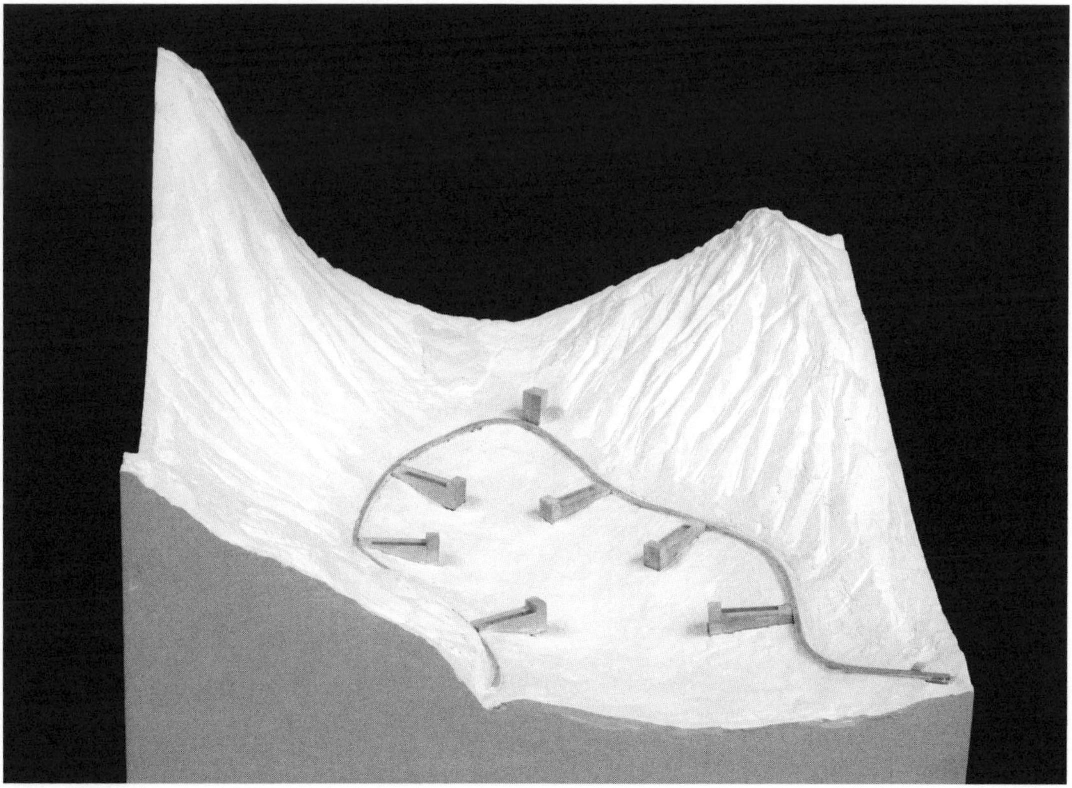

[117]

[118]

[119]

143

Model Construction Site

[121]

[122]

pour the concrete. Sometimes the geometry even requires the model to have some reinforcement. The model is remarkably close to reality!

Buildings can be cast or formed. Formable materials such as clay or plasticine enable a truly artistic approach to be taken to architecture, which accounts for the popularity of this method in the experimental phase of a design. Clay naturally comes to mind. It is one of the oldest basic materials in the construction industry and offers a haptic, tactile experience for the user. The shaped mass dries in air and can be remolded after the addition of moisture. Ceramics are created by firing the material in an oven.

Plasticine, which is relatively solid and dimensionally stable at room temperature, is easy to process because it deforms when warmed. It also supports the experimental approach, because the initial model can be changed by addition or subtraction but the whole effect remains homogeneous.

[118]
Plaster: colored by adding pigment, glycerin soap to represent water, 1:20

[119]
Plasticine is the traditional modeling material in architectural model making

[120]
Concrete: cast building model – in combination with a landscape chiseled out of porous concrete blocks

[121]
Clay: three-dimensional model, 1:20

[122]
The designer explores on a small scale in the model how the whole building is put together by joining individual parts, just as it is at full scale.

Making the model

Making every architectural model is an experience. The knowledge is derived not only from the three-dimensional experience for which the model is created. The act of building also contributes to this knowledge. What is the sequence? How is the work done on the "model construction site"? Just as in everyday practice, the architect, who may also be the "craftsman" during the model making phase, works from the drawings. A miniature, a building in miniature, arises step-by-step from the design.

Procedure

Architectural models are created in many different places. Students make them either in the drawing office or in model making workshops during their courses at universities. In architectural design offices, the interest in model making is more from the practical angle. Some offices do not work much with models, if at all, which means they are not usually to be seen and do not contribute to the working atmosphere. Large offices, on the other hand, have a corner for model making or perhaps even a workshop where students provide the model making skills. Then there are the professional, freelance architectural model makers, who are seen in the greatest numbers in regions where their potential clients – large or small architectural offices – have established themselves. Architectural model makers are often carpenters by trade, or have a creative educational history, but there are also architects who, after graduating, concentrate solely on making buildings at a small scale. This is certainly the most readily comprehensible route to a model making career.

University architectural faculties, offices, model making studios – all of these places may have "construction sites" for small-scale architecture.

How is an architectural model created in practice?

Model making usually follows the same basic procedure, which is usually not without similarity to building the final design. The first requirement is for drawings, which arise from the design for the model. These drawings either appear on the workbench in physical form or are fed into a machine as digital data. It is better if the model is at the same scale as the drawings, because then there is no need to convert dimensions. If a model is built by hand alone then the drawings can be used as templates from which each part can be produced. The facade, for example, can be placed on the modeling material, marked through with a tracing wheel and cut precisely with a modeling knife. The chronological sequence in the model workshop is as follows:

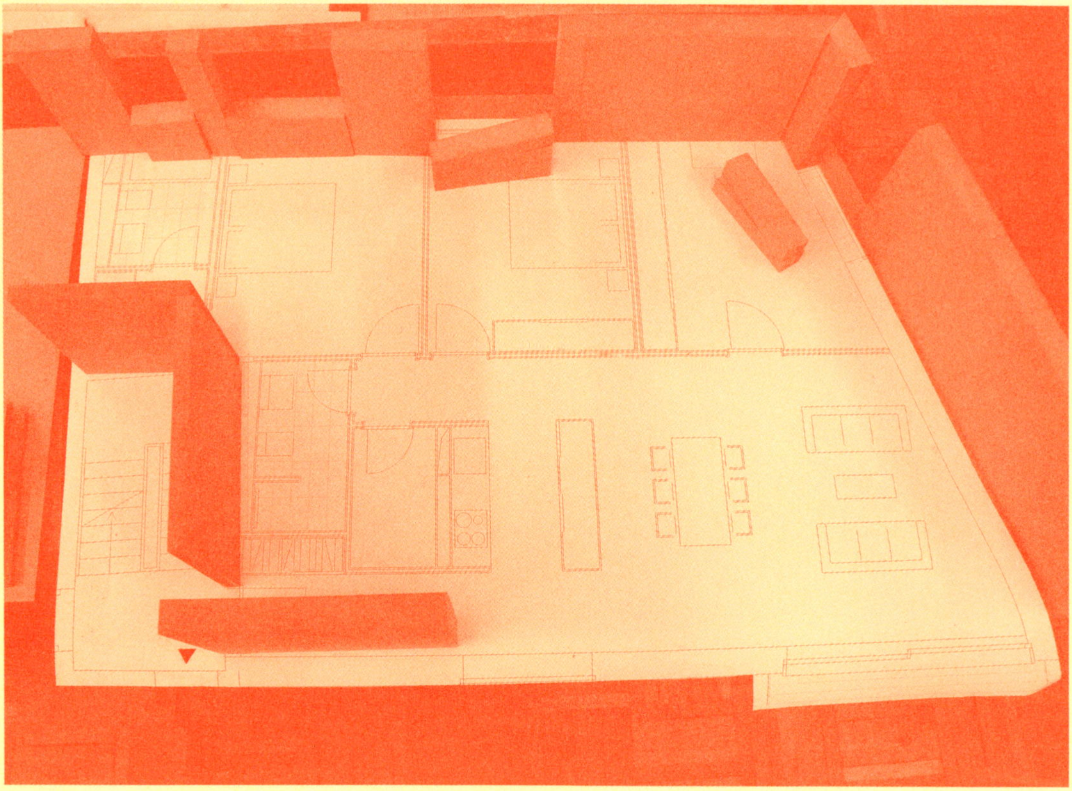

[123]

[124]

Typical work stages in model making (the detailed steps depend on the type of model)

The architectural design / concept
Workshop drawings for the model building site Design concept for the model
Making the mounting board Making the individual parts of the model (external and internal walls, ceilings, roof parts)
Transfer the floor layout onto the mounting board, mark the fixed points
"Building carcass" → Put together the parts on the mounting board or separately
Prepare and fit filigree details
Introduce staffage in the form of made-to-scale accessories Trees, figures, vehicles, further specific details
Color / color coatings Spray the whole model with varnish
Completion Lettering / model photographs / packaging

[125]

The setting is the mounting board

The big difference compared with reality, in the real world the land on which the planned building is constructed is already there and just has to be arranged to suit. In the model, this setting itself must be communicated and made before anything else. In university courses, students always breathe a sigh of relief if the surroundings to be modeled consist of a flat landscape, because they know they will finish this task quickly. The mounting board – a stiff, strong board in the simplest cases – represents the surrounding landscape. The model maker need only place the contours of the plot onto the board and then continue with the building itself. There is much more of a challenge and work involved with a building placed on sloping ground. A contoured mass of material is placed upon the mounting board to represent the topography. Not infrequently, making the surroundings of the building in this case involves more time and uses more material than the object to which it later provides the context. The topography is usually made up of layers on the mounting board with the result that the four edge faces of the board itself remain in view, while all other parts are filled with material or concealed in some way.

[123]
Model construction site: the model arises from the actual drawing.

[124]
Model construction site: every detail plays a role in design and construction, just as with the real building.

[125]
Model construction site: the model develops spatially in the third dimension from the floor plan drawing.

[126]
The mounting board can be made as a type of plinth to enhance the presence and effect of the model.

[127]
Architectural models of an uneven site are made up layer by layer, usually with concealed voids to save material. 1:200, gray paperboard

[128]
In this detail, it is apparent that abstraction using layers to represent the natural shape of the ground requires viewers to exercise their power of imagination. 1:200, gray paperboard

[127]

[127]

[128]

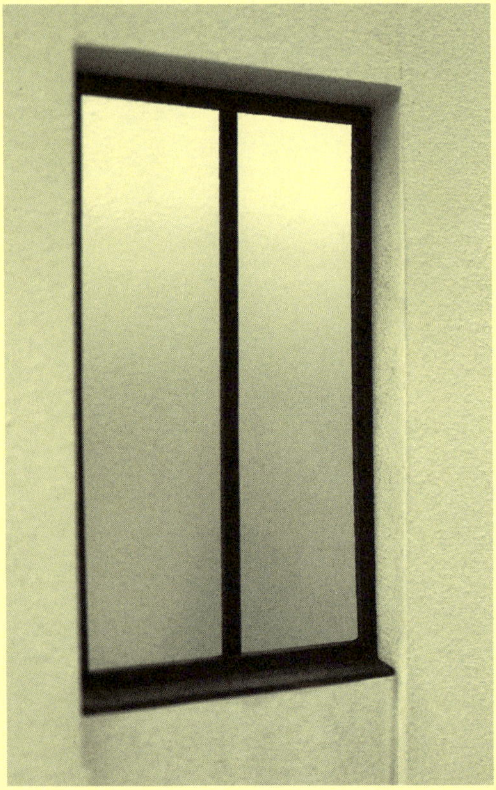

[129]

[130]

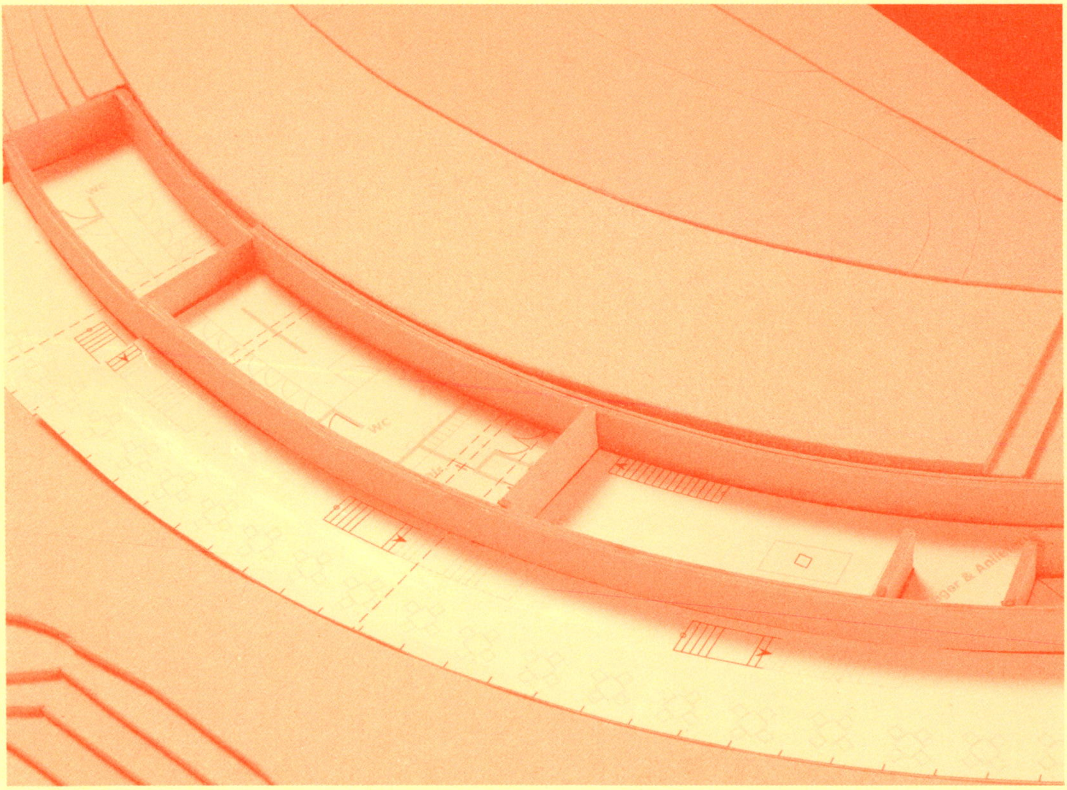

[131]

[129/130]
In terms of how it is made, every architectural model is a prototype of a modular system, the parts of which are assembled to create the building.
[131]
It is essential with site models that they are made to allow the "building excavation" to be added in stages.
1:200, gray paperboard

There are many ways of treating the edges, usually borrowed from furniture making, including applying the model material to the edges as a veneer so that the board disappears completely. Alternatively, the supporting board can be articulated like a tray as an independent element of the model.

The mounting board format is related directly to the position and area that the building will later occupy. The larger the board, the more the viewer can consider the context of the location into which the architectural design is inserted. The question of side ratios and proportion is linked with the physical characteristics of the architectural design. A building with a square footprint, for instance, should be placed on a square board. Alternatives to the square include a rectangular golden section shape or a 1:2 side ratio, which is usually an acceptable format. If the building stands freely on its own, then the opposite advice applies, i.e., the area of the board should coincide with the plan area of the building. The surrounding urban landscape can be intentionally omitted or shown later in a separate urban planning model. Depending on the choice of scale, the model may also be shown in section. Here as well, the question also arises of how much of the surrounding context to show.

Many different types of board materials may be used for the mounting board. Most model makers use wood-based boards such as medium density fiberboard (MDF). However, many other strong, stiff boards, such as laminated board or corrugated cardboard (depending on the format), are available.

Making the individual parts

The model maker works with the model just like a carpenter, who glues individual parts together in the workshop and assembles them later at the installation site. Walls, ceilings, columns, roof elements, windows, doors, and all other components have to be made specifically for the model and then assembled into the whole object.

Transferring the information from the drawing can be done using analog methods such as marking the intersection points of all drawn lines with a tracing wheel or needle, joining the points up with thin pencil lines and cutting out the required parts workpiece by workpiece. The following shortcut can be useful. Simply take a print of the CAD drawing and stick it to the material with adhesive tape. Then use a sharp knife to cut along the lines, thus saving all the work and eliminating the risk of errors in transferring the information. The modern version of this uses digital machines – CNC routers or laser cutters – to produce the components accurately and quickly out of the material.

The model maker should make frequent checks on the dimensions of the individual parts to make sure that no design errors have been made.

An area of interest is how to form the corners that are bound to occur when two walls meet at right angles. The simplest way is by a butt joint, which unfortunately reveals a cut edge. A more elegant solution is to form a miter (45°), which ensures that the corner looks the same from both sides.

With facades, the architectural design components are reduced by abstraction often to a simple relief with openings giving an effect of their depth into the surface. In practical terms, this means making the facade component in two layers, i.e., the holes are cut in the front layer and a second layer out of the same material is glued behind the first.

Modeling the surrounding landscape

In addition to the components for the actual building, the parts for the surrounding landscape also need to be made in advance. This is done by dividing the topographical heights into layers and building them up in the material used for the model. These layers are also taken from the location plan at the same scale and transferred onto the material – by analog or digital means – and cut out. It is best to mark and cut them out in the correct order to help ensure that no mistakes are made when gluing one on top of the other. The model maker can contribute to material savings when making the landscape model by leaving a void inside a hill, for example, or filling the void with a cheaper alternative such as PS rigid foam.

[132]

[133]

[134]

[135]

[132]
Figures in plastic at different scales and undertaking different movements populate the architectural space. 1:100
[133]
On a more abstract model, people are shown in silhouette, perceivable at a second glance. 1:100
[134]
People and everyday objects (accessories) explain and support the message of an architectural model. 1:50
[135]
Miniature model vehicles impressively convey the scale of the architecture. 1:500

As with individual parts, it is worthwhile incorporating later details at the same time. The routes and edges of roads can be carved out with a utility knife or engraved with a laser cutter onto the landscape model.

Joining the parts

After all the parts have been made, they are put together piece by piece in a previously thought out construction sequence. This is to determine whether all the parts should be permanently and unchangeably glued to one another, or whether a certain amount of flexibility is desirable by being able to remove some of the important parts, yet still have them fixed together. This has the big advantage that viewers can see the interior. The model also remains modifiable if particular components (facades, for example) are installed loosely and can be replaced, allowing different options to be tried out on the model.

The same principle applies to town planning models. The topography of the city is made as a permanent mounting board and the individual buildings – insofar as this flexibility is required – are temporarily fixed in place using insertion fittings or double-sided adhesive tape. It is a model of a building‘s surroundings that is made available to several architects as a common basic design element, the area of the model on the site of the designed object is inserted as a loose and replaceable area of the surface.

Staffage

Even architects do not always find it easy to visualize the actual size of a building from an illustration or drawing. When looking at the building carcass for the first time, clients often say that they had imagined its size to be different to what it actually is.

Models miniaturize reality and people do not have the experience to relate the model world to reality without points of reference upon which to base their perception. These points of reference are supplied by staffage.

In order to make the link between the model and reality, model makers use various inserted objects that the viewer recognizes, trusts, and is familiar with at full size as fixed points of reference. This

[136]

[137]

[138]

information makes the scaled-down representation comprehensible and legible. The size of an entrance, window or the dimensions of architectural details are easily imaginable.

Miniaturized people

What role do these fixed points of reference play? They are items that have no major or ancillary significance to the design and its architecture but are necessary to the model to complete the picture. Small-scale human figures provide the best impression for the viewer's imagination because everyone has an idea of their own height and can relate this to the model.

Modeling figures are available in all scales as injection-molded products and show lifelike people in various positions. A more abstract representation is as silhouettes, or at a scale of 1:200, two vertical grains of rice glued one on top of the other provide an abstract interpretation of the human body. Nothing should be left to chance in the placing of the figures in the model. The most important places in model space, for example, the entrance, should be occupied with figures, so that the staffage can also convey the attractiveness of the planned building.

Everyday objects

Depending on the purpose of the architectural design, "furnishing" the model with items relevant to the building's future use gives the best impression of its size and scale. A garage or a street scene are

[136]
Furniture to scale and inconspicuously positioned in the representation of the space gives lay people a precise impression of a room. 1:20

[137]
Where the natural surroundings are important in an architectural design, they should be placed appropriately in the foreground of the model. 1:200, Iceland moss

[138]
Treetops made from steel wool; branches and trunks from wound steel wire. 1:200

[139]
The creativity of many model makers is exemplified specifically in their abstract interpretation of trees: treetops made from sea moss, trunks from wooden rods. 1:200

[140]
Trees made from foam with holes cut in it, painted, 1:200

[1431]
Trees in the form of objets trouvés from nature, dried leaves, 1:200

[142]
Stepping away from naturalism: trees made out of circularly wound wire, 1:200

[143]
Frequently used: trees made out of yarrow, 1:200

[144]
The material used and how it has been processed basically define the model.

[139]

[140]

[141]

[142]

[143]

[144]

immediately transferable into reality through the addition of small model vehicles. In the context of transportation, as well as cars on roads, a model of an airport would not be complete without planes nor a ferry terminal without ships. Interior models at a scale of 1:20 or 1:10 have furniture appropriate to their use to express the spatial scale. The interior of the restaurant cannot be expressed properly without thought and representation of coordinated items such as tables and chairs. In houses, the viewer gains a better idea of how or whether the bedroom will work if the bed is shown in the correct position.

Trees and plants

Representing elements of nature, most commonly trees, is worthwhile not only in open space and landscape models of any scale. Hardly any model can dispense with this atmospheric ingredient, even if it is intended to be suggestive, because the size of the trees in the model often provide a preview of what they will be like in two decades.

Deciding on the right form and material is not without difficulties. Spheres, rods or improvised bunches of steel wool are abstract strategies to represent natural objects in a convincing way. They should correspond with the design of the other parts of the model. Another way is to use natural objects or plants. A tree is represented with a tree. It could be a delicate twig or a dried, thin-stemmed plant that corresponds closely in height and spread to the real tree. In every case, whether abstract or natural, trees and plants emphasize the character that a model seeks to convey to the viewer.

Staffage or kitsch

Because its use changes the expression of the model, not every model maker automatically reaches for staffage. In certain circumstances, it can reduce the level of abstraction or striking effect of the model. Objects that give an idea of scale are always something to do with the architecture of the model itself. On the one hand, they are a familiar and obvious element in the representation and can enhance the model. On the other hand, staffage should be introduced only if it has a contextual relevance to the expression of the model and is not just an incidental ornament. In the worst case, there is the risk of achieving the opposite effect with staffage, i.e., the expressive power is weakened if the viewer cannot see the form of the facade because the model maker has obstructed the line of sight with trees. Trees should only be used in the representation if they support the spatial concept in some way or other. If this is not the case, they should be left out because the old maxim still applies: Less is more!

Tools

Without tools nothing can be produced or manufactured, let alone built. Every trade has its own characteristic tool and this is just the same for the model maker. A collection of handy tools is sufficient to make concept and working models quickly and effectively while studying or in the architectural design office. As the demands on the quality of models rise, so do the required capabilities of the tool.

Basic assortment

For many people, model making is a hobby and therefore must be pleasurable. A not inconsiderable number of architectural students blossom for the first time in their studies when they put the pencil to one side and take a tool in their hands and find themselves sawing, filing, drilling, cutting, and gluing instead of drawing for a good part of the day. An architectural career combines both aspects, the theoretical and the practical, and model making manifests itself in the latter. What hand tools are used to make architectural models? What is the most effective way of organizing a model making workplace? What methods are recommended for model making while studying and in practice?

In addition to drawing equipment, a selection of important utensils is required to process simple model making materials.

[145]
Plants as part of the architectural concept, dried flowers, 1:20
[146]
Analog tools in architectural model making

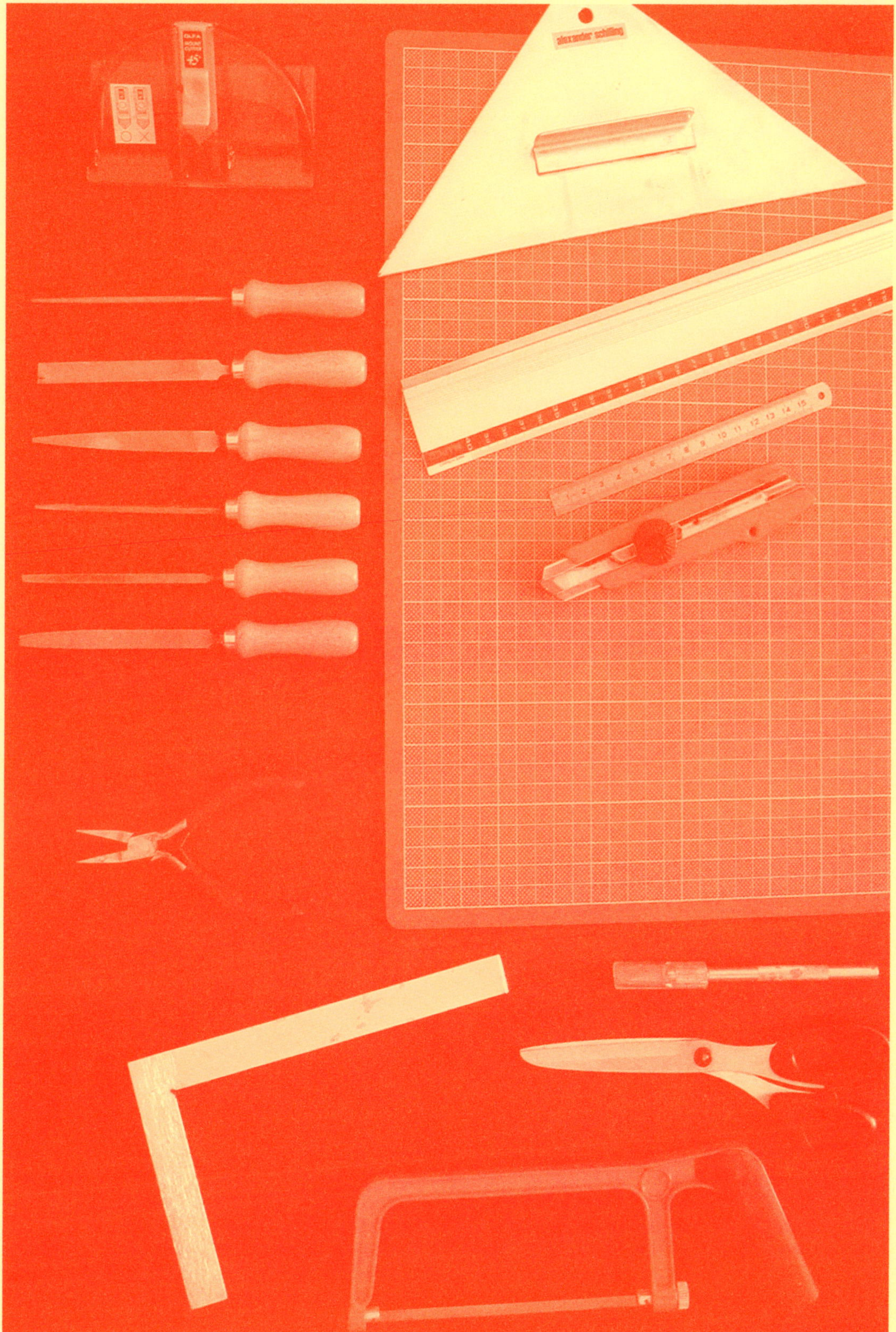

[146]

What basic tools belong in the model maker‘s toolbox?

Requirement	Suitable tools
Transferring the drawing onto the material	• Tracing wheel • Acetone with a cotton rag • Compass • Ruler and triangle ruler
Cutting	• Modeling knife • Scissors • Cutting ruler (with hardened steel edge) • Cutting mat
Gluing	• Wood glue (white or animal glue) • Universal adhesive
Sawing	• Hand saw, with a choice of blades for wood, metal, and plastic
Abrading	• Sandpaper (coarse – medium – fine) • Files
Measuring	• Ruler • Architect's scale (triangular scale ruler)
Color coating	• Acrylic paint • Spray paint (matte or shiny) • Clear varnish • Oils

Workplace

A large table similar to a drawing table provides an adequate workplace. It must be strongly built and stable so that it can support heavy models and allow the use of large machines. A vacuum cleaner is extraordinarily helpful because many activities on the model generate lots of dust and dirt. If all this is vacuumed away, no particles remain to detract from the effect of the finished model. Working on the model construction site handling wood, plaster, paint, or varnish can be a dirty job. Therefore, in a modern workshop, it makes sense to keep the dirty tables away from those where people are working with paper, cardboard, and filigree components, but most of all transparent plastics, which are extremely sensitive to dust. In every case, the table tops should be covered with a cutting mat – as protection and as a working surface – on which the modeling knife can be used. The workplace also needs glare-free artificial light so that the model maker has no difficulty in seeing the fine detail on the model.

Cutting

Typical steps in creating a working model: a sharp modeling knife and a cutting ruler are ideal for cutting and joining material to make a simple three-dimensional model of walls and ceilings out of gray or beige model-making card. In a process which is easy to implement and achieves relatively accurate results, it takes very little time to project the idea from the architectural design to the model. The modeling knife is an irreplaceable tool for this job, because it can be used on a large number of different materials. The modeling knife works using a simple principle; it is inexpensive and available in different versions with, for example, pointed or flat blades. A modeling knife especially designed for model making should always be used. A high-quality product is preferable to a cheap carpet knife from a DIY store. The cutting blade should sit firmly and precisely in the handle so that it does not wobble when cutting thicker paperboard. More force is used to cut thicker paperboard, therefore model makers must find out by trial and error which modeling knife feels more comfortable in the hand and suits them best. Like the pencil, which transfers the design out of the head directly onto the sketch pad, the modeling knife cuts the idea out of the material.

Every architectural student has to cope with the perils of this object, i.e., using the modeling knife could not be easier, but it is equally easy for users to cut themselves. The sharper the blade, the better the modeling knife cuts through cardboard and the more readily it cuts into the skin. Careful cutting and circumspect handling of the modeling knife are required to reduce the risk of injury. The stress of an impending submission date and the hectic activity of model making are dangerous and often lead to minor accidents.

In addition to the modeling knife, which is the traditional and most often used cutting tool, specialist shops also offer special versions. Borrowed from the world of medicine, a scalpel is a favorite tool of graphic artists and model makers because of its extremely narrow and sharp tip. Scalpels are a great help, for example, when working on the finest details or cutting out extremely small openings in the material.

Gluing

Gluing is a science in itself. The pitfalls here arise from the huge number of possible permutations of the parameters involved, that is, material A needs to be permanently and strongly bonded with material B. What adhesive is suitable for this? Complete familiarity with these substances is required to avoid chemical incompatibility between solvents and model materials, which may cause damage to the workpiece or the connection simply to fail. Universal adhesives, as the name suggests, are adhesives suitable for general use. They are also known as all-purpose glues or adhesives. If the product information indicates no restrictions, then the adheive is capable of bonding two different materials together. The most popular among these is wood glue, which can be used for woods of all types, wood-based materials and paperboards.

Adhesives play a part in most connections in architectural model making. Screwed, nailed or push-in connections are seldom used to assemble the individual parts into the complete model. As is the case with all adhesives, they have to be used correctly. A frequent example of incorrect use – with reference to the size of the contact surfaces – is applying too much adhesive. If a mason were to apply mortar to a brick in the same relative proportions as adhesive is applied to surfaces in a model, then the brick would drown. Model makers are recommended to pay attention to the amount of adhesive they use and apply little, in fact, very little adhesive, as it will always be enough. One trick employed by the model maker is to visit the drugstore and buy an ordinary syringe fitted with the largest diameter needle and use it to apply the adhesive. With some sensitive materials, the adhesive swells out of the connection and leaves behind dirty marks.

The method of cutting and gluing can produce very good results. A further advantage is that the model maker is not dependent on having access to a machine or a model making workshop. The models produced in this way are simple and fulfill the purpose. The materials used are correspondingly inexpensive and not difficult to procure.

Adhesives and their range of application

Adhesive (description)	Properties	Range of application
Universal or all-purpose adhesive (tesa or UHU)	• Synthetic resin adhesive, mostly containing solvents, transparent and viscous • Short curing times, achieve high strengths after a few minutes • Slightly irritant to the skin and respiratory system • Resistant to aging • May form threads during application, which leave behind a stain • Some are not suitable for PS rigid foam (act as solvents)	For gluing all kinds of materials to one another: • Paperboard to plastics • Wood to plastics • Various plastics together • Metals, glass, textiles, ceramics, porcelain, cork, etc.
Wood glue (white)	• Animal glue, a natural water-based product • Cures by taking up water from the surrounding material • White, pasty consistency in the liquid state, cures milky-opaque to transparent • Relatively long open time, during which the parts can be moved and their positions corrected (with the exception of quick-drying wood glue, which reaches its specified strength in 3 to 5 minutes)	• Excellent for all types of wood, wood-based materials, cardboard, and paperboard • For spot-gluing • The parts must be pressed firmly together to make the connection • Gluing large surface areas of wood together is done with a press, otherwise the high water content in the adhesive would cause the fibers to swell and warp the surfaces • Not suitable for materials that do not allow the adhesive to take up moisture from them (metals, plastics)
Contact adhesives (e.g., "Pattex")	• Contact adhesive, contains solvent • Relatively long open time, the connection is made when the two surfaces come into contact with one another • The adhesive bonds with itself. The surfaces of the parts to be bonded are painted with adhesive, exposed to air, allowed to dry and then pressed together • High contact pressure is crucial to the strength of the bond • Use only in well-ventilated rooms	• Excellent for full-surface bonding, for example, for raised-relief models or doubling up parts. May form threads during application, which leave behind a stain • More expensive than comparable processes because the surfaces to be bonded have to be fully covered with adhesive • The surfaces do not distort because the adhesive contains very little moisture • Can be used on wood, cardboard, most plastics, metals, and ceramics

Adhesives and their range of application

Adhesive (description)	Properties	Range of application
Plastic-bonding adhesives	• Runny, clear, solvent-based adhesive • Applied thinly on one side, the adhesive is spread like a film over the surface to be glued • Mostly suitable only for a specific group of plastics • The principle is based on the adhesive dissolving the surface of the material, which produces a form of welded connection • Short open time for joining the parts • Surfaces must be clean (free of dust and grease)	• Suitable for many thermoplastics such as polystyrene, PVC and PMMA (acrylic glass) • Unsuitable for PE and PP • Can be used to bond with non-plastics in some cases. Performs better than universal adhesive with plastics
Superglue	• Transparent, very fast-drying adhesive • Non-dripping, viscous consistency • For quick and lasting bonded connections • Contact with the skin and above all the eyes is dangerous	• Ideal for connections that cannot be held together and therefore require instant curing of the adhesive • Like a universal adhesive, it is suitable for many materials and combinations of materials
Spray adhesive	• Colorless, UV-resistant adhesive that comes in a spray bottle • Transparent to almost invisible on application • Hardly seeps into paper • Sufficient open time to correct • Avoid inhaling vapor, spray outdoors	• Ideal for all large-surface bonding and laminating applications, simplest way of creating layered models • Laminating may cause the supporting material to distort slightly. Balancing a front layer with a similar layer of the same material at the back is recommended when making a panel

Adhesives and their range of application

Adhesive (description)	Properties	Range of application
Two-component adhesive	Solvent free adhesive based on epoxy resin supplied as two parts: • base and hardener • The two components are mixed in the correct proportions immediately before use and must be processed quickly • Short open time, up to a maximum of five minutes • High final strength, rapidly achieved • Accepts extremely high loads	• Mainly used for bonding hard and solid materials to achieve a high-strength connection Suitable for most materials: • wood, metal, stone, concrete, glass, porcelain, ceramics, rubber, plastics such as rigid foam but not PE, PP
Rubber cement	• An adhesive made from natural rubber and organic solvents • One-sided application for use as a mounting adhesive, usually for collages by graphic artists • Elastic, viscous material, can be dissolved again in the dried state and removed from most substrates without leaving a residue • If applied to both parts, it creates a permanent bond	• Perfect for experimental work, collages and working models • Suitable for most materials
Solvents	• Solvents bond with the substrate through chemical reactions (dissolving the surface of the material) • Pressure is applied to weld the surfaces together and achieve a homogeneous connection of the previously individual parts • Irreversible connection Example: • Dichloromethane (methylene dichloride) • All organic solvents are very harmful to human health!	Suitable for gluing plastics, mainly: • polystyrene, acrylic glass, and polycarbonate

Adhesives and their range of application

Adhesive (description)	Properties	Range of application
Adhesive films and tapes	• Double-sided, usually transparent films or tapes • An alternative to fluid adhesives, because they are applied dry and do not adversely affect moisture-sensitive materials • Immediate bonding effect when the parts are put together	• Can be used for bonding large surfaces of materials of all types because the connection is mechanical • Plastics such as PP and PE, which cannot be bonded using fluid adhesives, can be connected in this way • Not suitable for spot-gluing

Adding to the basic range of tools

The model maker's toolbox is always expanding due to a steady flow of models having their own, additional requirements in terms of tools. The many different techniques and methods of model making bring with them the need for a large pool of tools in order to be able to tackle every job. A sensible approach is to limit the range of tools to those which are important and worthwhile. Every domestic kitchen cutlery drawer has a knife that can cut almost everything and some seldom if ever used specialist utensils that were bought for a one-off task and since then have remained unused. It is the same for the model maker's toolbox. In this case, it is better to borrow a tool from a workshop or a colleague for such single uses.

There are no limits to model makers' creativity when developing their own working aids, tools, and methods. When faced with prefabricating a large number of identical parts (columns, facade profiles, steps on stairs, etc.), it is worthwhile putting more thought into the process. Templates are helpful to transfer dimensions from the drawing 1:1 into the model and, for example, to ensure consistent distances between columns or walls. Model makers often feel the need for a third hand with which they could grip an object. Clothespins can prove useful. They can hold objects just like two fingers, for example, if glue is not curing fast enough. Another option is to use removable adhesive tape or, for larger pieces, fix them temporarily in place with screw clamps, which leaves the hands free for the next step.

[147]

[147]
The disk sander is a useful machine for architectural model making.

Additional model making equipment

Requirement	Suitable tools	Use
Cutting	• Scalpel and graphics knife • Side cutters and pliers	• Cutting out precise and fine detail • Shortening metal profiles
Gluing	• Special plastic-bonding adhesives • Rubber cement • Adhesive tapes and films	• Solvent and bonding action are compatible with the selected plastic • Repositionable (advantageous for working models) • Used mainly when materials are incompatible with fluid adhesives and for full-surface bonding
Sawing	• Metal saw • Fret saw	• For cutting fine metal and plastic profiles to length • For freehand shaping of plywood and veneers
Abrading	• Files • Rasps	• For cutting fine metal and plastic profiles to length • For freehand shaping of plywood and veneers
Woodworking	• Chisel • Hole punch	
Measuring	• Calipers • Steel rule	• Precise measurement to an accuracy of up to 0.1 millimeter • Scale up to 0.5 millimeter
Color coating	• Thin paintbrush • Masking film	• Applying color by various techniques • Stuck in place over the non-coated areas

Additional model making equipment

Requirement	Suitable tools	Use
Other tools	• Tweezers	• Helpful when holding and positioning very small pieces
	• Brackets	• Holding parts in place until the adhesive has cured
	• Screw clamps	• Stabilizes the workpiece during modeling
	• Rollers	• For pressing flat workpieces together when laminating or gluing

Machines

In addition to simple manual tools, model workshops also contain a series of useful machines that are indispensable for model making. They are recommended for processing harder and stronger model making materials, such as wood and metal, because they make cutting and shaping these materials much easier.

Saws

Wood has long been one of the traditional materials for producing beautiful models and it requires cutting and shaping using traditional machines. Primary among these machines are various types of saw, which are used to cut boards, veneers, and above all blocks of wood. Model makers work on much smaller workpieces than a carpenter, therefore saws are the right size of machines for the smaller-scale activities of model making.

A micro table saw can cut small components and wood profiles precisely to size. Because most of these table saws allow the blade to be tilted, they are very well suited for making small wooden blocks cut at an angle to simulate a sloping roof. The blade can be adjusted to set the sawing depth, which allows thin grooves to be cut in a surface to represent texture. Furthermore, every table saw has a longitudinal and a transverse stop to guide the workpiece precisely over the saw table. Because materials have different properties, such as thickness, the speed of the saw blade can be adjusted to suit.

Another important type of saw is the bandsaw, which – as the name suggests – has a continuously looped blade with saw teeth on it. This type of saw is excellent for shortening and shaping profiles and boards. A perfect saw for coarse work.

Many workshops also have a scroll saw. This type of saw works in principle as a mechanical version of a fret saw. A fine, linear saw blade is moved up and down by a motor to allow curves and free-form shapes to be cut from flat material. A textbook example of its use is the organically shaped layers of a topology model in wood.

This saw is mainly used on wood and wood-based materials, but it can also be used for many more purposes. With the appropriate saw blades, it is capable of processing many metals and most plastics in a similar way.

All saws have one thing in common, namely, the user must be extremely careful and concentrate when using the machine and be comprehensively instructed in advance by the workshop management or machine expert on how to avoid accidents. A short length of wood should be used as a working aid to keep hands a safe distance away from the saw blade when cutting tiny workpieces.

Drills

There are various types of drills for processing model components. Most of them are capable of boring holes of different diameters into the material with a view to creating a strong, durable connection between two workpieces. A good example is the circular columns that are inserted into sockets in the floor or ceiling, where they form a solid connection. By drilling the holes precisely, the parts fit together tightly, which can also mean savings in the amount of glue used. Another common use for drills is to make the holes for inserting the trunks of the model trees. It is important for trees to be firmly fixed into the model landscape so that they do not fall over during transport or if the model is subjected to vibrations.

Accurate guiding of the drill bit is essential when using a drill. The drill bit must move down exactly perpendicular to the workpiece. For this reason, many workshops do not have drills that rely on the hand to guide the drill bit; they have drills that sit in a drill stand with a drilling table that fixes the workpiece in position and can be set precisely at any required angle and stopped at the correct depth.

Architectural model makers can use micro drills, which are the equivalent of normal-sized drills but they are fitted with a micro chuck to mount drill bits of three millimeters diameter or less, right down to below one millimeter.

Sanders

Most sanding is done on wood. Using a sander makes working on the model tremendously easier compared with manual sanding. This is particularly true with hardwoods, where sanding by hand with sandpaper is an extremely thankless task. Sanding is a means of refining a sawn surface and achieving the envisaged final form of the workpiece.

In principle, any sander can be used with sandpaper specifically suitable for the material, be it wood, metal, or plastic. Sandpapers are graded using a unit called a grit; sandpaper described as 60 grit is very coarse, abrades away a thick layer of material and leaves a coarsely textured surface. The sanding marks in the material left by the rotating sander are very visible. Sandpaper graded as 240 grit is finer and creates a surface texture that feels smooth to the touch. Grades of 1000 grit or finer are used for plastics and metals. Wet-and-dry sand paper is used particularly for plastics because the high speed of the sander creates an enormous amount of heat, which requires the surfaces to be cooled with liquid to prevent the material from melting. Generally, the user must work with care when sanding wood to avoid the hot surface of the material turning brown or black and making the air in the workshop smell slightly but noticeably burnt.

The ubiquitous disk sander consists of a sanding disk, which acts as a backing to the sand paper, and a sanding table, which sits in front of the sanding disk. The table can be adjusted to vary the angle it makes with the sanding surface so any form of flat, angled workpiece can be sanded.

Other types of sanders include oscillating and orbital sanders.

Hot-wire cutting machines

A hot-wire cutting machine is a precision cutting tool for all materials that can be cut by the application of heat. The term “hot-wire cutting machine” is a logically correct description for these devices, however, one manufacturer‘s proprietary product name, “Styrocut,” has established itself as the generic name for these machines. Some architects simply call them hot-wire cutters, because this perfectly describes the principle of how they work. The hot-wire cutter is actually not much more than a fine metal wire through which electricity flows. The current, transformed down to a low voltage, causes the wire to become hot. In this state, the wire cuts blocks of material out of polystyrene rigid foam boards very quickly and without a sound. Many urban planning (working) models have been made using this method over the decades. The wire is tensioned perpendicularly to the working surface of the machine so that the thick rigid foam boards have only to be pushed through to the stop. Thicker boards must be pushed more slowly past the wire or the current suitably controlled. However, the machine has its limits, beyond which the wire burns out and the cutter must be restrung.

Hot-wire cutting machines are partially responsible for the presence of odor-neutralizing curtains in model workshops, because the peculiar smell of the fumes released when cutting polystyrene due to the action of heat is something architecture students never really forget.

Soldering irons

Soldering is a traditional method of joining metal wires to produce a neat and professional result. Structural models or models that seek to represent a load-bearing structure made from filigree members are often made as soldered-wire models.

The most suitable device for doing this is the electric soldering iron. The active part of these devices is the fine point on the soldering iron bit, which applies heat to a solder bar or wire to liquefy the solder – the connecting material between the two wire ends – and thus form the connection.

Other machines

In addition to the tools mentioned above commonly used in architectural model making, there are other useful machines.

Impact lever shears, often seen in metalworking shops, are used for accurate and linear cutting of metal sheets of various thicknesses and formats.

Electric planes and planing machines are commonly used in wood processing to reduce the thickness of the cross section of pieces of wood by removing layers of material.

Spray guns used in combination with a compressor to provide the required supply of compressed air are used to apply color coatings to models. The pigmented medium is sprayed through the fine nozzle of the gun onto all surfaces of the model to leave a homogeneous, thin color coating.

Digital model making

The computer is taking over complete working and manufacturing processes in model making, just as it is doing in many other fields. The development of digital and digitized methods began some years ago and have become state-of-the-art in model making workshops as well as in some architectural offices. Very high investment costs are usually required to install digital machines, but as is the case with furniture making, where the carpenter who does not have computer-controlled manufacturing machines is no longer competitive, the freelance architectural model maker is also reliant on this technology. Most university architectural faculties have this sort of equipment in their workshops, which is to the advantage of the students.

CNC routers

Modern machines are computer controlled with the data from the drawings being directly processed and converted for the machine. In the same way that CAD applications have digitized drawings, this will be the logical consequence of the introduction of computer-controlled methods into model making. Model components are made by computers. They can be reproduced in endless numbers and with extraordinarily high precision to look perfect to the human eye. Furthermore, the process of making these objects is considerably shorter than by analog or conventional processing.

In technical terms, a CNC router (Computerized Numerical Control) is a device that works in three directional axes to cut the required workpiece on its cutting surface. It operates similar to the way a plotter produces a drawing, except that it has a third dimension in addition to the X and Y axes. The computer-controlled routing and engraving head carves the lines and shapes configured on the computer screen out of the material. It can be set so that it does not completely cut through the material, but merely engraves a relief in the board.

The actual work of the model maker is reduced to programming the process. Because the CNC machine is controlled through a dedicated application, the data from the drawing produced by the CAD application must be converted to the standards used by the cutter. The vector graphics of the drawing must be converted before CNC processing begins, in order to ensure that it contains only the information upon which the processing is based. All superfluous lines and objects must be deleted.

Additional information must be provided, for example, indicating whether and how the cutter operates into the depth of the material. This is done by incorporating level information into the cutting data. The head itself has a specific material thickness and therefore, in the interest of precision, it is important to indicate whether the drawn line lies on the inner or outer edge of the cutter head

[148]

[148]
CNC router in a model making workshop

or on its central axis. If this is not done, there will be differences in the dimensional accuracy of the workpiece in the millimeter range. As with plotters that produce digital drawings, the user must understand how the CNC router works, how to use it and recognize the ever-present pitfalls. Trial prints are made of drawings to allow fine adjustments of the graphical components. The same approach is recommended for digitized model making.

The router has its limits, which are related to the options for processing each type of material. Not all materials are suitable for processing with CNC routers. Aluminum, brass, steel, and stainless steel in the form of metal sheets or plates (usually up to a thickness of 3 to 5 millimeters) can be cut. Higher quality, cast acrylic glass can be processed in layer thicknesses of approximately 10 millimeters; the same applies for plastic such as polystyrene. Also worth mentioning in this context are wood-based materials such as laminated glued plywood (multiplex birch plywood), or MDF.

Laser cutters

Now an even more modern device has appeared that is used far more frequently than the computer-controlled router, i.e., the laser cutter. As the name suggests, a thin laser beam cuts what has been programmed out of the material with absolute precision. In contrast to the principle of routing, which carves out some parts of the material, the laser cutter uses heat. The cut line is burnt out of the material in the truest sense of the word.

The translation of the digital drawing into the standard used by the laser software is as uncomplicated as it is for the CNC router. Because the laser head moves in the X and the Y directions only, the depth of the cut into the material is determined by the strength of the laser. This depth is specified simply by giving the lines in the original drawing different colors and assigning these colors within the software as either being partially or fully burnt through the thickness of the material. The file format can be, for example, a PDF file.

Compared with a CNC router, the laser beam is much more precise, with a cutting width in the region of 0.1 mm. This precision is particularly apparent in the formation of a negative corner. The router head is round and its radius determines the radius of the internal corner. The laser beam, on the other hand, does not suffer this limitation. The corner is produced with sharp edges.

The laser cutter is impressive to use because it cuts its lines much quicker than the CNC router and can be used on a much more diverse range of materials. The use of the machine is limited only by the size of its working area. The maximum size of the workpiece depends on the design of the laser cutter. The maximum material thickness also differs from machine to machine. A little model making design trick can help with this restriction. Cut a number of copies of the workpiece out of thinner material and then bond one on top of the other in coincident layers (sistering). Every method has limits to its feasibility; it is the architect‘s job to come

[149]
Laser cutter: the digital drawing provides the template for the machine.

[150]
Laser cutter: inserting the material.

[151]
Laser cutter: the laser beam reproduces the lines of the CAD drawing precisely and engraves or cuts the material.

[152]
Laser cutter: the workpiece is cut in a few seconds.

[153]
Laser cutter: sharp edges, turned dark by burning in the case of most materials, are typical of laser cutters.

[154]
3D plotter: the plotter works by a process of addition

[155]
Digital tools enable a precise representation of details at the smallest scale. Silhouette figures made in polystyrene, 1:200

[156]
Digital tools excel in their precision and speed, especially on workpieces with fine details

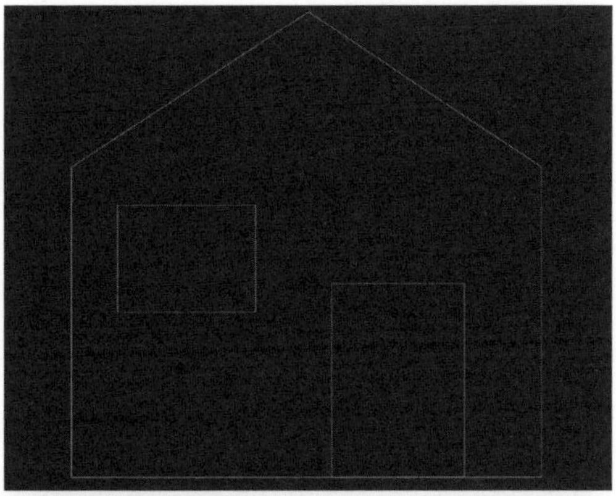

[149]

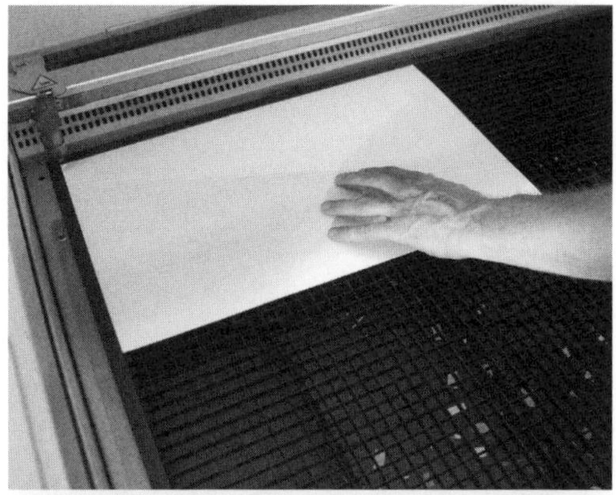

[150]

[151]

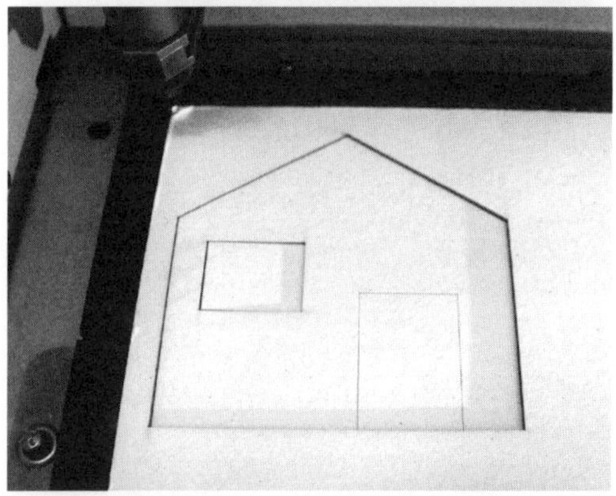

[152]

[153]

[154]

[155]

[156]

up with clever ideas to overcome these restrictions.

Before the actual model making starts, the user should experiment with the laser beam and make samples and trial cuts to find out exactly how the material behaves under the laser beam and whether the results are likely to be satisfactory. In university architecture faculties that have a laser cutter, students make fairly frequent use of the technique. The speed at which material can be processed is unsurpassed and leaves every analog method in the dust. However, what impression does an overprecise model make? Instead of working with simple techniques to build a coarse and imprecise working model, the laser beam is switched on without hesitation and a concept model is produced to the standards of a presentation model. The simplicity of the laser cutting process causes the user to forget just how quick and easy it is to cut things by hand.

A common expression refers to something characteristic of the laser cutter, the devil is in the details indeed! Wood pulp board and wood-based materials are popular for model making. However, the heat of the beam turns the cut edges of these materials dark brown or black and the surface looks as if it has been burnt. This begs the question as to whether having very dark edges compared to the rest of the material on the model really creates the desired impression. Does it make a difference whether the window reveals are dark and contrast with the facade or appear homogeneous and monochrome? The model maker can either accept the extra work and sand the color off or retouch these dark areas with color, at least on the presentation model. Is it right that the design of important details be compromised because of a machine's special characteristics when processing materials? In some cases, the viewer associates an image of a fire-damaged ruin after looking at a lasered building model.

3D plotters

Another concept of digitalized model making is the 3D plotter, which "prints out" the complete three-dimensional object. This technique is also known as stereolithography. The printing process is extended by the third dimension and the result is a spatially realistic object. Until recently, this technique was merely a marginal note in the broader field of architectural model making, however this process is becoming increasingly popular. The method originated in prototype construction for industrial and product design. Because an architectural model is also a prototype – although not at full scale – it is not surprising that this device is now also used in architecture.

The principle is the reverse of CNC processes. Instead of a subtractive process in which material is removed to create the required shape and geometry of the object, its shape is built up additively as more and more material is added. The result, without any intermediate processing steps, is a complete three-dimensional workpiece, which is the three-dimensional print out of the model already stored in the computer. The method is based on the principle of placing very thin, fine individual layers of the material successively one on top of the other. Either liquid or solid materials are amassed to the dimensions and shape required by the data in the computer. The materials are usually plastics, synthetic resin, or ceramic compounds, but also metals. The bonding of one layer upon the other is achieved by curing or melting by means of chemical or physical processes.

The unusual aspect of these models is that they come out of the machine virtually finished and the sculptural nature of the material results in its needing very little or no further processing or coating. The equipment used for 3D printing is still very expensive and the size of the chamber in which the printing takes place limits the size of the model.

[157]

Combination of analog and digital

Since being introduced, digital machines have opened completely new fields and possibilities for representation in architectural model making. In addition to the ability to program once and then repeat the manufacturing process as often as necessary, these new techniques have also led to new developments in the field of mold making. Complex geometrical textures, which would be very expensive or impossible to achieve manually, can now be represented.

From a practical point of view, these machines are safer to work with because safety guards ensure there is no direct contact with dangerous machine components. The amount of dust and dirt that people are exposed to is less than that in a conventional workshop. Architectural model making would be unthinkable today without the use of CNC machines. The reduction in the amount of work involved and the huge scope of possibilities are enough to convince even the most ardent traditional model maker. However, some of these idealists regret the lack of the recognizable individual style that sets a model apart. This aspect should not be interpreted as nostalgia: the result is that all the objects presented look perfect. They have become an expression of the end in itself rather than the experimentation that should take pride of place in the creation process.

In order for the possibilities of manually produced work not to disappear from view completely, an effective course of action could be to combine different ways of processing materials with one another to retain the individuality of the model maker and incorporate the oft-mentioned handwriting style. As is the case with built architecture, buildings gain their expressiveness through a combination of traditional processes with modern techniques. Wood can be precisely processed with a laser and then the surface given an interesting texture by manual processing to create a much more distinctive result.

[157]
3D plotter: A machine that can produce a complete three-dimensional model without any further manual interve.

[158]
Even in the digital age, wood excels through its natural uniqueness.
Curjel & Moser, model of Luther Kirche, Karlsruhe, 1907

[158]

[159]
Usually a neutral black background is used to document the model photographically.

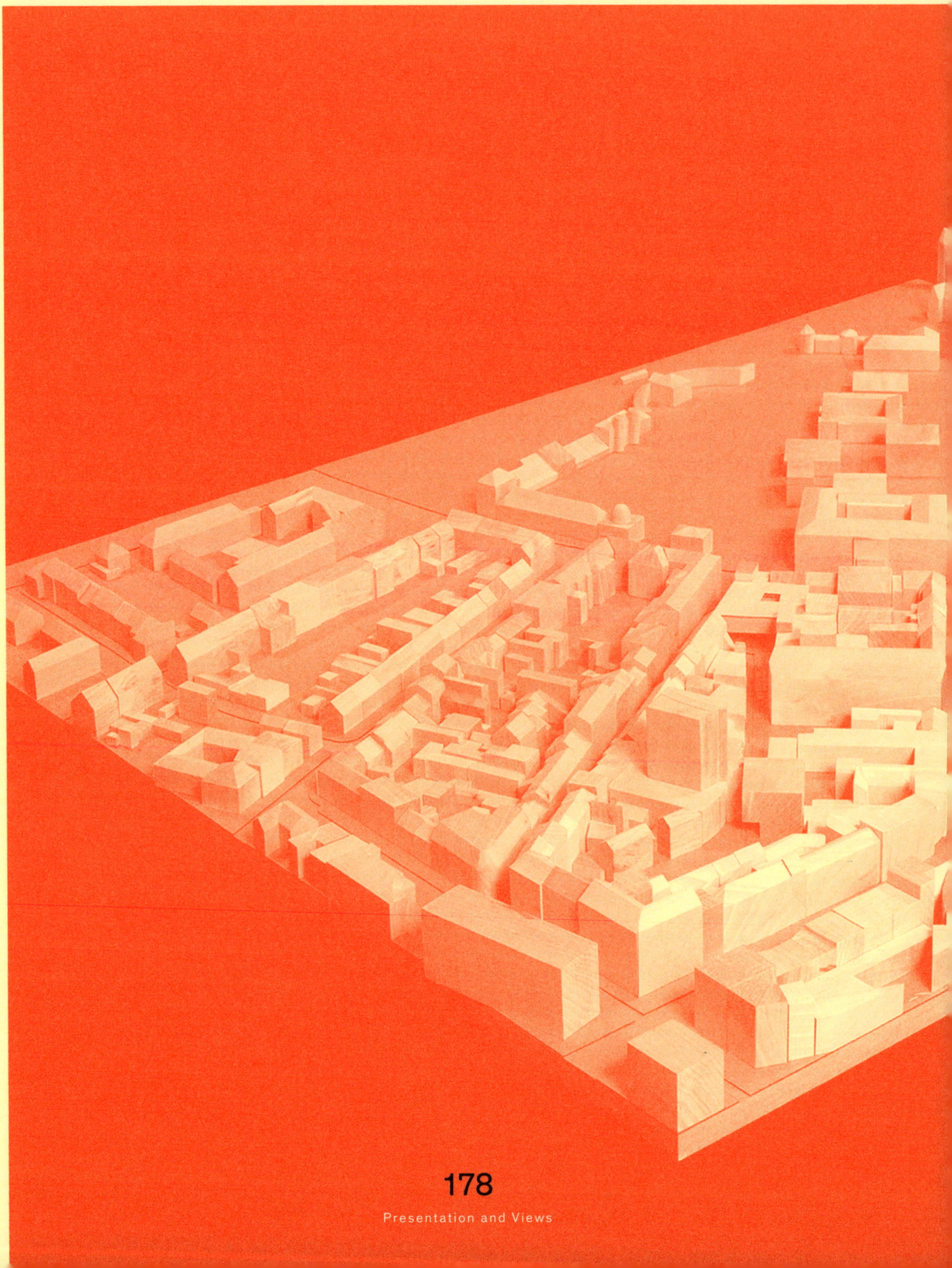

Presentation and Views

6

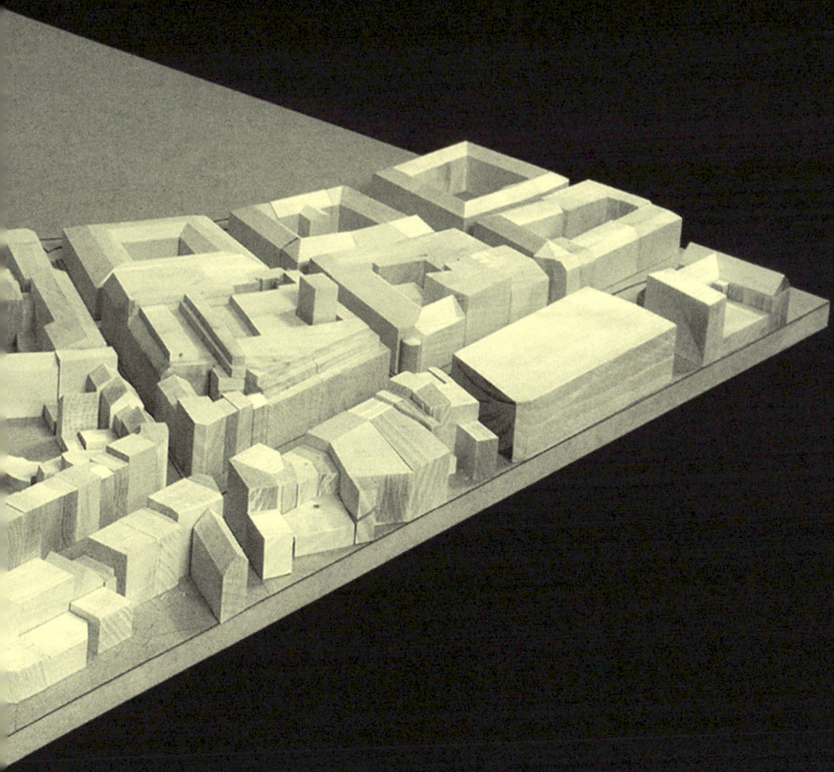

The architectural model has been finished. The little building is complete and the architect and model maker are satisfied with the result. Now the model is put to its intended use and can fulfill its *raison d'être.*

[160]

[161]

Architectural models in the eye of the beholder

Representations of architecture are often seen as part of the architect's idiom. The architect is the author of the design and speaks through this means of representation. The model is one of those idioms that are one thing to learn but another thing to use grammatically and rhetorically in the correct manner. This chapter considers the rhetoric of the model, the eloquence with which it can now speak for itself.

Of course, a model should always be able to speak for itself. It enhances and expands the possibilities of making architecture tangible and – as a result – able to be communicated and promoted.

How autonomous should the model be? Is the expression of a design exclusively the business of the model or should it be read and understood in the context of drawings, images and, where necessary, other types of media? Does it speak for itself or accompany and support the architect at a presentation or a talk? How the model will be used should be borne in mind when first considering whether to make one. Only in this way can its design and materialization be optimally selected to produce the desired effect.

But how does a model convince the viewer? Models in general have the power to fascinate. People often find miniaturized representations of our environment and our everyday activities particularly appealing.

It is no coincidence that the almost kitschy models of aircraft, ships or miniature railways reminiscent of our childhood are so popular. Lay people can draw other expectations from a model of a building, for example the model of a detached house at a scale of 1:50 in the window of the local real estate agent. Naturally, it is shown in a green meadow alongside a tree.

Architectural models make themselves understood in a different way. As abstractions, their concept is based on the principle that every model has its own identity and expression. That is, anything insignificant is left out or simplified, which leaves the significant as the focus of the representation. This approach leads to success if the model is viewed by the target group for which the model was created.

Models are used in design presentations at universities and schools of architecture. Here it is important that students deliberately integrate the model into their presentations, place it actively and assertively at the focus of perception, explain the content directly on the model, and exhaust every opportunity to convince the viewer of the quality of their work. It must be said that models in academia often play the role of stepmother to the drawings displayed on the presentation board. However, unless special emphasis is placed on the model in an assignment, it receives only peripheral attention in the critique of the student's work. The responsible party here is the author of the design, who does not adequately recognize, if at all, how the project could benefit from the model.

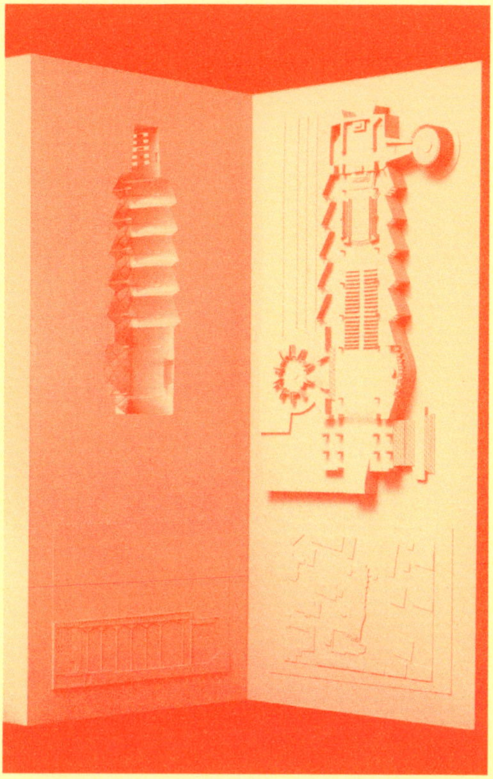

[162]

[160]
An eye-catcher draws the beholder attention to the content of the model.
[161]
The model's multilayered design communicates its content literally on several different levels.
[162]
The model can be a medium for spatial and architectural expression while, at the same time, an object with its own design quality.

[163]

What is the practice in architectural offices? In Germany, architectural models play a fundamental role in everyday architectural design in only a few professional offices. The reason for this, of course, is that design and the communication of architectural concepts constitute only a small part of an architect's work. In these offices, it is frequently left to trainees to quickly glue a model together when and if one is required by the client. Models are expensive and therefore have to be specifically commissioned and paid for. Negotiating generally comes before model making, unless the architect is so convinced of the potential of communicating through the model and specifically adopts this medium to successfully and convincingly represent the design idea to the client. Both sides stand to benefit from the use of models. It is essential to point out that working with models delivers commercial advantages because the competing methods of representation, such as the digital model, also involve time, effort, and expensive software or tools. Many architects say that clients show hardly any interest in drawings in the absence of a model at meetings where designs are discussed, but are fascinated and excited by a model of their building.

In what surroundings is the model most effective? How best to go about creating and, in particular, presenting the design idea to the viewer in a model is a question not without significance. The model maker should certainly put thought into how the object will be perceived. In architectural drawings, great emphasis is placed on ensuring that every sheet is horizontal, displayed in the correct order and at eye level. How should the model be positioned? Frequently, the model is simply placed on a table. In the case of landscape and urban space models, the insight into the spatial context gained from a bird's eye view is also worthwhile. With individual buildings and especially with models of interior space, this is not a recommended viewpoint from which to perceive the spatial expression of the design idea. The viewer should instead be given the opportunity to engage visually with the model at eye level, relative to the scale used.

Models depicting a large area built to a small scale, for example urban space and landscape models, have buildings that are not very high and therefore create an effect similar to a three-dimensional drawing or display board. This offers the alternative of attaching hooks or similar devices and hanging the model vertically. This assumes the wall or other support is capable of safely carrying the load.

If the architectural model is to take on a larger significance, for example, because it is intended for presenting the design of a public building and may be exhibited for a long time in a town hall foyer, then it is a good idea to manufacture a plinth or base to suit the mounting board in both quality and style at the same time and treat it like a piece of furniture. The model with the substructure made to cover the mounting board should form an integrated unit and provide an air of elegance and lasting value. In favorable circumstances, this approach can enhance the design concept. In the case of a tall, slender structure, a similarly proportioned plinth can also strengthen the perception of the design idea.
Events with an architectural theme or exhibitions about the works of great architects in museums are increasingly providing opportunities for presentations

[164]

[163/164]
The model has a cast plaster surface with a rigid polystyrene foam core and no visible mounting board or subconstruction. It is part of a series of architectural models depicting individual buildings of an ensemble in sequence, with each building set in the landscape around its location. Each model stands on a frame made to measure by a metalworker out of welded square hollow steel profiles to raise the series of models to the correct height for the exhibition.
Landscape model, 1:5000

[165]

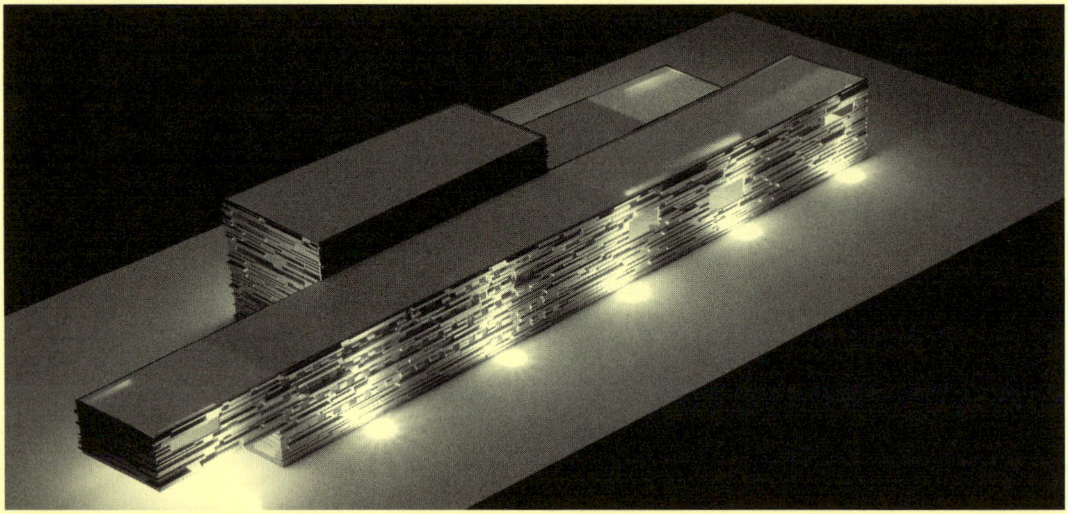

[166]

[167]

and displays of work. Models of the architecture involved are an important part of every exhibition concept. Experience proves that visitors show most interest in the models on display simply because they communicate their content visibly and impressively. More recently, museum exhibitions have clearly demonstrated that models come closely behind the built architecture in their powers of expression.

In the context of an exhibition, the model is not only highlighted by a plinth or an appropriate piece of furniture, it can also be protected from dirt and damage by a transparent guard similar to a display cabinet made of glass or acrylic glass. Models are made up of slender and often delicate parts, which means they may be very fragile. Some models are of historic value and any damage could be irreparable. Exhibits behind glass, in a display cabinet or case seem to gain a special significance of their own by the distance from the viewer usually imposed in a museum environment.

Model photography

The completed architectural model speaks for itself and serves the purpose for which it was made. This three-dimensional object can be experienced physically and the model's presence alone is enough to entice the viewer. As well as being available to view directly, it can also be used as a photo model. It provides the opportunity to create photographic versions of the represented space. This leads to a further added-value of the model, i.e., it can be used as the basis for perspective representations, whether to supplement the drawings or for use in brochures and portfolios.

After completion, architectural models are often photographed for archival purposes and to have the object available in an additional, more easily handled image format. Just as the architectural photographer captures the work of the architect in photographs following the completion of a building, the same applies to completed models in most architectural offices and in the photographic workshops of architectural faculties at universities. Models are worth conserving for posterity. These images are outstandingly suitable for self-advertisement and references. Because the size of a model with the mounting board makes it easier to capture on camera than the completed building, model makers can normally take their own photographs.

In addition to providing photographic records, the model can generate added value in other ways, for instance, the creation of perspectives in photographic form. Here the model really becomes a photo model and is the center of attention. It is an effective and proven additional means of creating photorealistic renderings. And an excellent alternative, particularly if the amount of effort involved in creating an effective and strongly expressive virtual image on the computer is taken into account. Derived photographically from the model, perspective photographs depict aspects of the content such as spatial relationships, materiality, surfaces, and not least the intended lighting mood.

As with model making itself, some familiarization with photography and handicraft techniques is necessary before taking the photographs. A good knowledge of photography is required by anyone taking these pictures themselves. Capturing this miniature world and the exact scenario in an image requires an adequate selection of lenses.

If the situation is more challenging, it may be necessary to work with a professional photographer. In the atmosphere of the photographic studio, the image is created under optimal conditions, which ensures the model is perfectly transferred onto the paper. The photographer must know exactly what the architect wishes to achieve with the model and for which group of viewers the photograph is intended so that the expression can be translated into the image. Being able to try out different angles in various lighting conditions is, of course, an advantage in determining the best settings. Models allow the camera to be set up on any side so that the architectural expression can be completely captured. In the same way as architectural photography, in addition to depicting the model as an

[165]
The architectural miniature is photographed – not in a neutral way, but positioned in the atmospheric context of its location.
[166]
Using artificial light to display the architectural model
[167]
The expression of materials in the light

[168]
Daylight creates the character of a space.

object providing information, the model photograph also has the task of promoting engagement with the expression of the idea that led to the creative process of design and representation in the model in the first place.

The architect uses the model images to call attention to the spatial relationships in the design. The design that is legible in the model is also communicated by the image. Perhaps the photograph succeeds in an even more obvious way in narrating the crucial design aspects that have been systematically accentuated in the model. The image works like a filter that draws the important content out of the model to make it more understandable. The architectural model is an object in the subjective perception of its viewer. Everyone who casts their eye over the model does so intuitively and with the benefit of their professional architectural insight. The model image is therefore easier to read, to understand, because it simulates a real viewpoint and communicates the architectural moment to the viewer. The architectural sequence is amplified and – through the use of light – raised if necessary to the level of exaggeration.

To repeat a point made at the start, an architectural model contains much more information about the design than any drawing, detail or perspective. In most cases, this is also the great, if not the greatest, advantage that the model has over all other methods of representation. However, it is also worthwhile, depending on the target audience, to use the model and extract the most effective expressions from the myriad of available information. Construction professionals find it easy to cope with and assess the content of the model. For clients and the lay public in competition award juries, however, it can be difficult to see and comprehend everything. This is where photographs of the model can help to explain the concept of the representation. The model maker can use photographs to control and – in a positive way – influence the viewer. The architect has control over the decision of how the design expression is communicated to those on the other side of the model.

How perfectly crafted – in terms of the photograph – the result appears depends on the quality and capabilities of the photographic equipment. The geometry of the model space and its physical dimensions dictate the requirements of the camera, the lens, and the mode of operation. In principle, taking a photograph of the model from outside is fundamentally different from creating an image of a model depicting interior space, which is much more complex and difficult to accomplish. The size of a model – relatively large or small – calls for a pragmatic approach to the question of how best to go about obtaining the images. Access to an architectural or photographic studio, where the architectural model can be highlighted by being placed against a neutral background and there is controllable lighting, makes the procedure easier. Many of the models shown in this book are produced in the traditional way against a black or light, neutral background in a photographic workshop. To achieve a pleasant contrast between the object and the surroundings, models made from light-colored materials are better photographed against a neutral, dark background, while light backgrounds are more suitable for models made from dark materials. Adjustable artificial light sources ensure optimal illumination of the object, ideally from the side and not from the front, to bring out the sculptural qualities of the model in the photograph.

If a studio is not available, a suitable site for photography may be improvised. Why not take the architectural model out of its normal surroundings and model making context? Just as the real building is expressed in a specific environment, it can be very helpful for the atmosphere that the model image is supposed to recreate if the model is set in surroundings that approximate reality. Models can be illuminated very well outside in the open air with the sky clearly in the picture so that the lighting conditions appear natural and authentic. In a similar way to architectural photography, daylight scenarios with clouds diffusing the sunlight are recommended so that the lighting of the model surfaces is softer and gentler. Hard shadows and overexposed surfaces (mainly with light-colored architectural models) can be corrected by processing the image, but only after a lot of effort. Natural staffage such as the surroundings, horizon, and the sky can lend an element of reality. If trees stand before the real window from which the view is generated, then the model can be positioned in front of a real tree. Because of the trick of perspective depth, it is not noticed in the later image that the model is really a miniature of reality, even though the tree and the sky are still their original size.

When building the model, the model maker should think about whether and how the model will

[168]

[169]

[170]

[171]

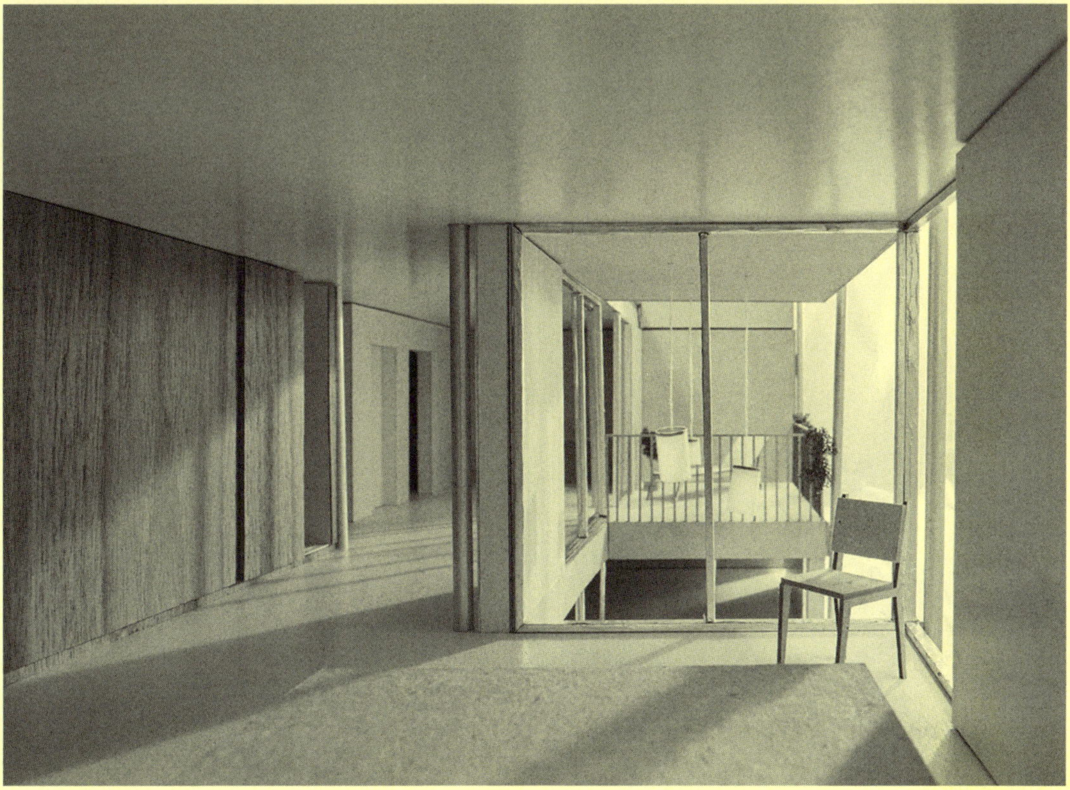

[172]

[174]

[175]

be used for photography, because the camera in its housing could be huge in the context of the model, depending on the scale selected. A good strategy for interior models is to incorporate removable parts or openings through which the lens can be pushed.

Another important aspect to consider with photography is the height of the camera. A bird's eye perspective is a good view for documenting the model, but the viewer is normally aware that it is only a model, not a building. The camera needs to be at eye level for the viewer to experience the architectural space. Setting this height to the similarly notional horizon line gives the viewer's perception a concrete reference to reality. In a scale 1:100 model, the image axis lies at approximately 1.70 cm above the mounting board. Thus the physical dimensions of the camera means it is already at the limits of use and the model maker needs to think about whether and how to create a recess in the mounting board for the camera. Only in this way will the photograph look to have been taken at the correct height and therefore produce a comprehensible impression of the space.

Should the image of the model be intended to explain the character of the space, then it is important not to become too involved with the mechanical and technical processes of photography but look for a fresh creative approach to achieve this intention. Making a conscious choice of the camera position with respect to the space in the model followed by experimentation with perspectives and different lighting moments will eventually create the ideal image.

Stepping back from these detailed considerations, it is worthwhile thinking in terms of what would be the best sequence of photographs for explaining the context of the model in a photo series for a specialist magazine. That would be one way of ensuring the viewer experiences the full content of the model.

When working on a design project, many architects keep a sketchbook in which they collect all their thoughts, ideas, and discarded considerations to record and document what went into the process. In a similar way, the creation of the model in all its metamorphoses and stages of development can be recorded with the camera. The experimental work on the model takes place in a long series of steps, with the designer thinking up variations and modeling them at various levels of detail at all stages of the project. The photographic image preserves these intermediate stages, because the model is constantly being rebuilt and modified.

Digitally optimized model images instead of renderings?

In what ways can the photograph of the model be used? In the age of digital photography, the image that the camera supplies is not the finished article. Most people have access to digital image processing software and can use this tool on their photographs. The main reason for processing the model image is to further improve its expressive effect. A computer is used at this stage to heighten and intentionally accentuate the content. In general, the main aim is to sharpen the image over the full depth of the depicted space. However, these tools can blur as well as sharpen to highlight certain parts of the space or have them retreat into the background of the viewer's perception, as required. In the case of architectural models, the surrounding staffage such as trees, people, or vehicles is still relevant for communicating the scale, but the user can choose to lower their resolution and have them appear as blurred objects in the edges of the picture.

Correction of any distortions in perspective that may have occurred due to the differences in size of the camera and the object is important in communicating the idea. The most important of these are lines and building edges that appear not to be vertical and should always be avoided in order to allow a satisfactory perception of the space.

High-resolution digital cameras have a special characteristic that calls for post-processing of the photograph, namely, the photographs produced by these devices are too good! The human eye is very forgiving of minor mistakes left here and there in the model by the model maker, for example flecks of glue that have not been properly removed from a room corner. Interestingly, these defects appear much clearer and are more obvious on the image because the camera exaggerates such faults. The photographs are very easy to retouch using image processing software.

Another topic which should be mentioned at this point is the color mode used for the photograph. A colored image will provide a more realistic reproduction of the model, whereas a monochrome photograph will bring the aspects of brightness and light, darkness and shadow into the foreground. Before digital photography became an everyday tool for representing architecture, most model images were black and white. Where the intention has been to reduce the number of different materials used in a model (monochrome models or models that simplify the materiality of the real object), an image taken in black-and-white mode is crucial to emphasize the abstraction that has already been made part of the model. In addition to the color mode, there are filters and processing modes that can be used in digital photography to give the model image an artistic flavor. One example, given here only to illustrate the possibilities, is the additional graphical effect of visible graininess.

The architect obtains photographic representations of his design from the architectural model, which he already has at his disposal. The photographs could be described as a valuable and reusable waste- or by-product of model making. These images could be considered as a feedback loop with two-dimensional representations of space being created by photographing the three-dimensional model. With designs that are considered to have complex geometries or shapes, it is often simpler to use a physical three-dimensional model to obtain perspective views instead of building a virtual three-dimensional model on the computer.

[169]
Model photograph with the photo model: digital photography allows a view into the miniaturized rooms.

[170]
With the help of image processing, the result communicates the impression of the room to the viewer.

[171–173]
Abstract at this scale, the images generated with the help of the architectural model communicate the important aspects of architecture: light, materiality, proportion, and composition. Interior models, 1:20

[174]
Architectural model: The viewer can see how the model is made and perceives its uniqueness from its style.

[175]
Rendering (visualization): Representation of detail better communicates the expression of reality.

[176]
Ludwig Mies van der Rohe, Farnsworth House, Illinois, 1945–50, building model, painted wood, 1:50

Outlook

Digitalization is continually changing everyday processes in the world of work. These changes are also affecting architecture in all areas where media are used to represent designs or completed projects. But what does this mean? What role can the physical (often referred to as analog) model assume now and in the future, and what parallel developments can supplement the model?

Architects first saw the computer as an interesting tool in the 1990s. The development started with the replacement of the drawing pen by the CAD program. In earlier days, a line began and ended with the flow of black ink on smooth tracing paper; nowadays this process has been replaced by two mouse clicks on the computer. The drawing is created far quicker and is, at the same time, more precise and reproducible. The computer turned the tools that served generations of architects and were a hallmark of their profession into antiquated museum pieces. Within just a few years, these drawing implements have completely disappeared from the consciousness of today's creators of architecture. It is not only the tools that have changed. Architecture has changed at the same time. Perhaps it is a fundamental trait of human nature to minimize effort and shy away from some decision making. How did architects draw the vertical and horizontal joints in masonry on facade elevations with such endless diligence in those days? Thanks to the computer, any pattern can be created at the click of a mouse. The enormous calculating power of the computer now allows architects to create shapes and systems that would have been simply unimaginable in the days of drawing by hand.

The effect on architectural model making has been similar but delayed. The wave of digitization did not dissipate before it reached the workshops of professional model makers and finally the schools of architecture. Why should this have happened? The obvious advantage was the technical possibilities of cutting out workpieces digitally. No more modeling knives or working by hand to physically guide the blade over the cardboard and make a unique model. This was replaced by the router and later by the laser beam, which is capable of cutting to almost immeasurable accuracy and at an incredible speed. A student would hesitate at designing a facade with a thousand window openings because of the thought of incorporating them all – very likely under time pressure – into the model. Cutting out minuscule openings to scale would be something that anyone would not rush into doing. How would that be done now?

Drawings have long since been produced only by computer in universities and professional design offices. This would not apply to the initial hand sketches, of course. In most cases, two-dimensional construction drawings and all the three-dimensional data of buildings are produced on the computer using 3D software. The computer beguiles architects because they have less need to think in three dimensions. Thinking structurally and spatially from a floor plan in order to produce sectional views is no longer necessary because the software can do all this for the user.

What are the effects of digital tools on model making? Something, if not everything, has changed in the approach to making a model and, as a result, in the effect the model exerts. The skill of the craftsman is still valued in built architecture. Joiners and cabinetmakers working in traditional skilled trades place particular emphasis on the quality of their work and the resulting product is unique to them. This craftsmanship is transferred into model making but with a difference, namely, the workpieces produced by digitized machines do not quite transfer the individual touches of their creator into the architectural model and look more like the type of construction kits supplied by one of the famous manufacturers of buildings for model railway systems. It is not reactionary to entertain the view that manual methods also have their uses in the digital world. This is not only because they are popular traditional skills, but also because they are obvious and equally justifiable methods of working alongside the new tools. In many cases, it can also be simply quicker to place a piece of cardboard on the cutting mat and cut out the required item than to produce a digitized drawing and send it to the machine. In addition, every discovery made using manual methods greatly benefits the model maker's awareness and understanding of the process. Every architectural student should have the experience of preparing a drawing by hand using a pencil or drawing pen. In the same way that every qualified chef should first make whipped cream with a whisk before using an electric mixer.

It is not only tools that were once analog and are now digital. Presentation media in architecture have also undergone an enhancement in the scope of use because of digitization. An enhancement that is also described with the term model, i.e., the three-dimensional model. This mode of model making involves designing the building in a digital drawing program by entering all the data for the components in three-dimensional format from the beginning. Whereas in earlier days, a wall consisted of two lines in plan, with the distance between them giving information about its thickness. In three-dimensional space, the wall is a complex component and requires its length, thickness, and height to be entered with reference to the appropriate axes from the beginning. The drawing is no longer called a floor plan. It is the view created by a vertical projection onto the desired plane from above. If the designer changes the type of projection, the computer generates the view, which may be a section or an elevation, from the available data. Therefore, the building exists as a virtual model.

This can be taken forward a further step during design by linking the information in the three-dimensional model with design information *that does not appear on the architectural drawing – Building Information Modeling.*

How do these two different types of model compare? Although they are not both used on all design tasks, one thing is already obvious, i.e., the digital model of a building extends and modifies the processes involved in the design of the building.

How important is the physical model in this changed context? Could the architectural model be regarded as outmoded – a model that has been phased out? This question should never arise if the architectural model is as described in this book. Returning to the characteristics of the physical model mentioned at the start, it can be concluded that the architectural model cannot be replaced. Without a replacement, it cannot be deleted from the pool of possibilities. The model retains its unique selling point that it represents the architectural space as a truly three-dimensional object in miniature. Physically accessible and touchable. Virtual models will be helpful and are a justifiable additional means of representation. But they should be seen less as competing and more as acting together in a form of synthesis. The two concepts of representation stem from different approaches. The time-honored approach of architectural model making will retain its power to fascinate as long as buildings continue to be designed and built. The forward-looking approach of the digital model helps to achieve other objectives, i.e., efficiency in the design process based on the principle of an intelligent process.

Conclusion

Students in undergraduate architectural courses engage with architectural space and elements starting from the beginning of the first semester. This engagement immediately involves the question of the best way to represent their ideas. Without models, this engagement cannot take place. Practitioners and students of this profession are set the following basic challenge: the design of space and its architecture. The architectural profession is changing. Technical advances and demographic change have always had immediate consequential effects on architecture. However, models have remained an effective method in architectural design throughout the ages. The methods of model making have developed in a strikingly similar way to real construction. New techniques have not spared the model making workshops and drawing offices of university faculties and this advancement is to everyone's benefit. The earlier chapters of this book have pointed out several times not only that the architectural model is an object depicting a miniaturized version of a real building, but also and more importantly that the processes of creating and interacting with the model are just as significant as its simulation of reality. People say that architecture is a mirror of the society in which it is created and the same can be said of the relationship between people and models.

Our fascination for models continues unabated. For designers, the model represents an important tool in their engagement with space and its proportions. Every line, every drawing of the design is visualized in three dimensions and made tangible only through the model. It encapsulates the relationships between drawings. Clients and nonexperts in architecture are quick to recognize the advantage of three-dimensional representation of space through the model. Visual thinking takes various forms. The model captures the attention of the viewers and places the expression and the effect of the design clearly and comprehensibly before their eyes. That is the benefit of the model.

What significance will future generations attach to architectural models? A quotation from the founding director of the Center for Art and Media (ZKM) in Karlsruhe, Heinrich Klotz, expresses how the traditional and progressive can always exist together: "Computer graphics has had as little effect in making painting superfluous as the coming of the synthesizer caused people to throw away their grand pianos."[1]

1) Heinrich Klotz (ed.): *Center for Art and Media Karlsruhe*, ZKM 1992.

Acknowledgments

For me, writing this book meant an intensive engagement with a subject that I have pursued with passion and commitment for longer than I have been involved with architecture itself. Even more valuable were the experience and knowledge I gained in researching and writing the book.

I would like to express my thanks in particular to the following people and institutions for their support, inspiring discussions, and suggestions for this publication:

Karlsruhe Institute of Technology, Faculty of Architecture, Karlsruhe:

- Institute of Architectural Design, Art and Theory, Building Theory Group, *Professor Daniele Marques* and *Professor Meinrad Morger*
- Institute for Building Design and Technology, Principles of Building Construction Group, *Dipl.-Ing. Thomas Haug*
- Institute of the History of Art and Architecture, Architectural History Group, *Dr. Dorothea Roos*
- I would like to thank you all for the images of exemplary models, most of which were produced in design and research projects in recent years as part of architecture courses.
- Master Model maker *Manfred Neubig* at the Study Workshop for Models for the valuable ideas about the craftsmanship involved in architectural model making
- Photographer *Bernd Seeland* and his team at the Study Workshop for Photography for their advice and assistance with many model images

University of Applied Sciences Karlsruhe Engineering & Business, Faculty of Architecture and Civil Engineering, Karlsruhe:

- Laboratory Manager *Thomas Brenner* of the Architectural Laboratory for his valuable ideas about craftsmanship involved in architectural model making and digital methods
- In the field of model photography, *Dipl.-Ing. Max Seegmüller* for the images of exemplary models, most of which were produced in design and research projects in recent years as part of architecture courses
- In the field of open space design, *Dipl.-Ing. Günter Mader* for the constructive conversations and the images of exemplary models

Gerstäcker-Bauwerk GmbH, Material for Model makers and Artists, Thomas Rüde, Karlsruhe for his advice on materials and assistance in photographing tools and materials.

Jannis Bruns, Karlsruhe for providing model photos.

Peter Hoffmann, Karlsruhe for providing model photos and digital perspectives.

Lisa Schneider, Karlsruhe for providing model photos.

Florian Weinmann – Gestaltung Modellbau Möbel, Stuttgart for providing model photos.

Meixner Schlüter Wendt Architekten, Frankfurt am Main for providing model photos and project images.

SAAI – Archive for Architecture and Engineering in Southwest Germany, Karlsruhe, Prof. Georg Vrachliotis and Dr. Gerhard Kabierske for valuable information and background to the history of architecture and architectural model making and model photos.

UAA – Ungers Archive for Architectural Science, Cologne, *Mrs. Anja Sieber-Albers* for providing model images.

Annette Gref of *Birkhäuser Verlag* in Basel for her support and inspirational guidance as the editor of this book.

Harald Pridgar for his wonderful graphic design and layout of the book.

And finally, I am particularly grateful for the boundless support of my family, who have patiently and lovingly accompanied the author on his journey. I found the peace for writing this book at the right time in the tranquility of the Friesian countryside in Friedeburg.

Further Reading

- Bert Bielefeld (Ed.), *Basics Architectural Presentation,* Birkhäuser 2014
- Oliver Elser and Peter Cachola (Eds.), *The Architectural Model: Tool, Fetish, Small Utopia,* Scheidegger & Spiess 2012
- Wolfgang Knoll, Martin Hechinger, *Architectural Models: Construction Techniques.* Deutsche Verlags-Anstalt 2006
- Ansgar Oswald, *Architectural Models.* DOM Publishers 2009
- Alexander Schilling, *Basics Modelbuilding,* Birkhäuser 2013

Image credits

Unless otherwise indicated, all images in this book were created by Study Workshop for Photography, photographer Bernd Seeland, Faculty of Architecture at the Karlsruhe Institute of Technology (KIT), Karlsruhe.

The following images were provided to the author by KIT, Faculty of Architecture, Building Theory Group:

p.4
"Hochhaus in der Frankfurter Senckenberganlage" (Skyscraper in Frankfurt, Senckenberganlage), 1964, Archive of Works by Egon Eiermann, photo: Horstheinz Neuendorff)

1
Charles Rennie Mackintosh, Mackintosh Building, Glasgow School of Art, Glasgow, 1897–1909, Seminar "Facades"

2
Andrea Palladio, Palazzo Chiericati, Vicenza, 16th century, Seminar "Facades"

3
Alte Pinakothek, Munich, 1826–36 and 1952–57, Seminar "Facades," Leo von Klenze, Hans Döllgast

22, 35
Design "Artwork," Elvira Leuschner

23, 24, 57, 168
Design "Bad am Bodensee," Jerónimo Haug

25
Design "Zahas Nachbarn" (Zaha's Neighbors), student coursework

29 (left above)
Design "Berlin," Julia Albrecht

29 (left below), 63
Design "Berlin," Stephan Dietzel

29 (righ above)
Design "Berlin," Timo Eisele

29 (right below)
Design "Berlin," Silke Wernet

31
Design "La Spezia," Marina Ruff

32
Design "Bad am Bodensee," Michelle Langer

33,34
Design "Transferzentrum" (Transfer Center), Mike Schneider

36
Rathaus, Göteborg, 1916–37, Seminar "Facades," Gunnar Asplund

37, 68, 69
Seminar "Dominikus Böhm," group work model

39
Design "Xbox," student coursework

40
Design "Landau Godramstein," student coursework

42
Design "Parkhaus" (Parking Garage), Stella Polymenopoulou

44
Design "Lissabon" (Lisbon), Daniel Albrecht

45
Design "Wroom," Chen Ji

46
Le Corbusier, Notre-Dame-du-Haut Church, Ronchamps, 1950–55, Seminar "Layouts"

50
Design "La Spezia," Iannis Piertzovannis

51
Design "La Spezia," Heinrich Töws

52, 56
Design "Landau Maulbeerbaum," student coursework

54
Design "Stadthaus in Karlsruhe" (Townhouse in Karlsruhe), Manuel Kratky

55
Design "Datscha," Marina Ruff

58
Historical front model, Seminar "Facades"

61
Design "Stadthaus in Karlsruhe" (Townhouse in Karlsruhe), Sojeung Shin

67
Design Paris, Gizzem Cinar

74, 75
Design "Reykjavik," student coursework

76
Design "Xbox," Cyrill Urban

79
Design "Lissabon" (Lisbon), Fabian Wieser

81
Design "XBox," Lucia Eichhorn

82, 83
Design "Xbox," Simome Rösner

84, 85, 86
Working models from classes, student coursework
87
Design "Artwork," student coursework

88
Design "Landau Godramstein," student coursework

89, 90
Studio space, 1st semester, group work

91
Model of Luther Church, model making workshop

92
Design "Casino Köln" (Casino Cologne), Anna Katharina Braune

95
Design "Artwork," student coursework

96
Design "Wroom," Cyrill Urban

118
Design "Bad am Bodensee," Florian Rothermel

119
Plasticine, student coursework

120
Design "Hotel Bad Gastein," Laura Bissbort and Anna Katharina Braune

121
Design "Cabanon," Moritz Schineis

127
Design "Drachenfels," Verena Fessele

128
Design "Drachenfels", Sarah Lehmann und Cristian Popescu

131
Design "Drachenfels," student coursework
132
Design "Kunsthalle Karlsruhe" (Museum of Art Karlsruhe), Matthias Spath

133
Design "Kunsthalle Karlsruhe" (Museum of Art Karlsruhe), Katrin Tilsner

134
Design "Berlin," Friedemann Jonas

136
Design "Stadthaus in Karlsruhe" (Townhouse in Karlsruhe), Sarah Moser, photo: Steffen Kunkel

137
Design "Casino," Friedemann Jonas

138
Design "Cannstatt," student coursework

139
Design "Drachenfels," Gergana Pantcheva

140, 142
Design "Drachenfels," Janna Tzoulakis and Madalina Marincu

141
Design "Elefantenhaus" (Elephant House), Birgit Rapp

143
Design "Sehnsucht" (Longing), Mirjam Martin

144
Design "Stabwerk" (Framework), Angelina Weigel

145
Design "Bad am Bodensee," Brigitte Kalausek

158
Wooden model "Lutherkirche" (Luther Church), model making workshop

159
Design "Kunsthalle Karlsruhe" (Museum of Art Karlsruhe), Carolin Brügge

162
Sir Basil Spence, St. Michael's Cathedral, Coventry, 1956-62, Seminar "Layouts"

166
Design "Sehnsucht" (Longing), student coursework

167
Design "Kunsthalle Karlsruhe" (Museum of Art Karlsruhe), Thomas Schmitz

170
Design "Stadthaus in Mailand" (Townhouse in Milan), Zhizhong Wang, photo: Steffen Kunkel

171
Design "Stadthaus in Mailand" (Townhouse in Milan), Valerie Faust, photo: Steffen Kunkel

172
Design "Stadthaus in Mailand" (Townhouse in Milan), Wiebke Weidner, photo: Steffen Kunkel

173
Design "Stadthaus in Mailand" (Townhouse in Milan), Steffen Hollstein, photo: Steffen Kunkel

The following images were made available to the author by KIT, Faculty of Architecture, subject area: Principles of Building Construction. The models were made by students as part of their coursework:

47, 59, 60
Design "Casa die Stefano. Ein Stadthaus für Mailand" (Stefano Residence. A Townhouse for Milan)

The following images were made available to the author by KIT, Faculty of Architecture, History of Architecture Group:

6, 7
Historic plaster model of Strasbourg Cathedral

8
Model Friedrich Weinbrenner, Local Parliament House, Karlsruhe, 1822

9
Models of designs by Hermann Alker

The following images were made available to the author by the Karlsruhe University of Applied Sciences, degree program: Architecture. The models were made by students as part of their coursework:

17
Model "Haus Schminke" (Schminke Residence), Hans Scharoun, Löbau, 1932–33

20, 176
Model "Farnsworth House," Ludwig Mies van der Rohe, Plano, 1950–51

18
Model "Haus Eiermann" (Eiermann Residence), Egon Eiermann, Baden-Baden, 1959–62

19
Model "Haus Tugendhat" (Tugendhat Residence), Ludwig Mies van der Rohe, Brno, 1929–30

21
Model "Design Landhaus in Backstein" (Design Country House in Brick), Ludwig Mies van der Rohe, 1924

97
Model in wood "Barcelona Pavillon" (Barcelona Pavilion), Ludwig Mies van der Rohe, Barcelona, 1929

The following images were made available to the author by the Karlsruhe University of Applied Sciences, degree program: Architecture, Open Space Design, Dipl. Ing. Günter Mader. The models were made by students as part of their coursework; photos: Günter Mader:

53 (above)
"Ikone der Gartenarchitektur – Al-Badi Palast Marrakesch" (Icons of Garden Architecture – Al-Badi Palace Marrakesh) Model makers Natalia Szymansek and Martin Weisshaupt

53 (below)
"Ikone der Gartenarchitektur – Patio de los Naranjos Zaragoza" (Icons of Garden Architecture – Patio de los Naranjos Zaragoza) Model maker Baris Wenzel

The following images were made available to the author by Lisa Schneider, architect, Karlsruhe:

30 (above), 117, 163
Master's degree project "Die Unausweichlichkeit des Raumes im Valle Meira" (The Inescapability of Space in Valle Meira)

164
As above, photo: Marlene Hübel

The following images were made available to the author by Peter Hoffmann, architect, Karlsruhe:

93, 174, 175
Postgraduate project "Inis Mór – ein klosterähnliches Refugium" (Inis Mór – a Monastery-like Refuge)

The following images were made available to the author by Jannis Bruns, architect, Cologne; all photos: Jannis Bruns:

30 (below), 41 (p. 59), 160, 161
Master's degree project "Ressource Raum" (Resource Space)

41 (p. 58), 49
Design "Space in Time"

64
Design "Ice Lab"

77
Undergraduate project "Wein mit Weitblick" (Wine with a Vision)

The following images were made available to the author by Valerio Calavetta, architect, Munich:

43, 126
Master's degree project "Wohnen im Wildpark" (Housing in a Wildlife Park)

The following image was made available to the author by Philipp Loeper, architect, Hamburg; photo: Philipp Loeper:

165
Postgraduate project "Meeresbad"

The following images were made available to the author by Christoph Baumann, architect, Büdingen; photos Christoph Baumann:

58
Design "Islamisches Gemeindezentrum" (Islamic Community Center)

The following images were made available to the author by Meixner Schlüter Wendt Architekten GmbH, Frankfurt am Main:

38, 70, 71, 73
Model Haus F (F Residence), 2005–07, photo: Meixner Schlüter Wendt

66 (above)
Dornbusch Church, 2004–06, photo: Christoph Kraneburg

66 (below)
Dornbusch Church, 2004–06, photo: Meixner Schlüter Wendt

72
Haus F (F Residence), 2005–07, photo: Christoph Kraneburg

78
Model study Haus Schlüter (Schlüter Residence), 2003, photo: Meixner Schlüter Wendt

80
Model study residential high-rise, 2012–16, photo: Meixner Schlüter Wendt

The following images were made available to the author by Florian Weinmann, Gestaltung Modellbau Möbel, Stuttgart; all photos: Florian Weinmann:

48, 65, 122, 135, 155, 156
Architecture, building models and impressions of the workshop

The following images were made available to the author by saai Archive for Architecture and Engineering in Southwest Germany at the Karlsruhe Institute of Technology:

4
Museum of Art, Mannheim, Hermann Billing, 1907, plaster model Atelier Billing, photo: Bernd Seeland

10, 11
Model Pestalozzischule, Karlsruhe (Pestalozzi School), 1915, photos: Bernd Seeland

14
"Hängehaus mit zentralem Mast und Zugseil" (Tensile structure with central pylon and guys), 1961, photo: Bernd Seeland, Archive of Works by Frei Otto

13
"Schlaufenstudie für eine Kirche" (Loop Study for a Church), 1964, photo: Bernd Seeland, Archive of Works by Frei Otto

16
"Haus Mohl" Karlsruhe, 1983, photo: Klaus Kinold, Archive of Works by Heinz Mohl

62
Kaiser Wilhelm Memorial Church, Berlin, 1959–61, photos: Carl Albiker, Archive of Works by Egon Eiermann

The following images were made available to the author by UAA – Ungers Archive for Architectural Science, Cologne:

5
Overdoor featuring the city relief of the Baroque planned town of Karlsruhe, Bernd Grimm, Bibliothek Ungers, Cologne, photo: Bernd Grimm

15
San Pietro di Montorio ("Tempietto"), Rome, Donato Bramante, Renaissance, Bernd Grimm, photo: Stefan Müller

Images by the author:

28, 94
Competition Keltenweg Nursery School, Baden-Baden, Schweikert Schilling – Architektur und Gestaltung, Karlsruhe, 2017

98, 99, 100
Images of model making

101–116
Images of model making materials

123, 124, 125, 129, 130, 146, 147, 148–154, 157, 169

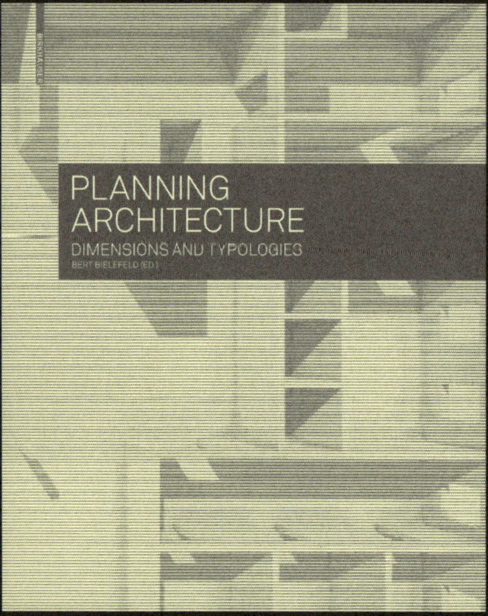

Planning Architecture

Dimensions and Typologies

Bert Bielefeld (Ed.)

568 pages, 1200 illustrations
978-3-0356-0324-8 (Softcover)
978-3-0356-0323-1 (Hardcover)

The book offers architects and students a thought-out planning tool, in which two main sections reciprocally complement one another: the “spaces” and the “typologies” between which the planner can flexibly oscillate depending on his or her plane of observation. All relevant planning information is presented in a detailed clear fashion, and in context.

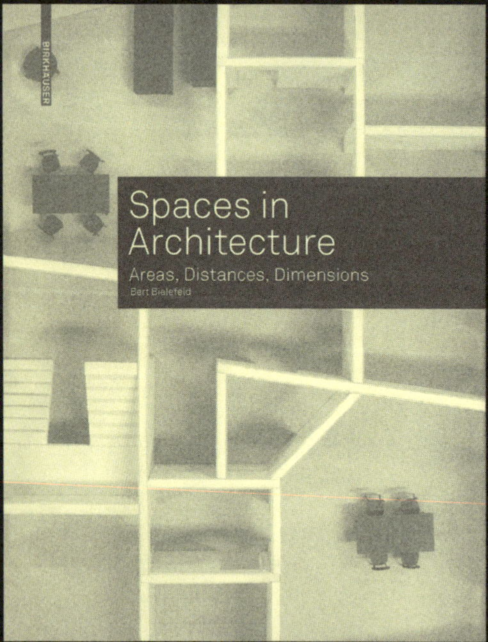

Spaces in Architecture

Areas, Distances, Dimensions

Bert Bielefeld

164 pages, 250 illustrations
978-3-0356-1723-8 (Softcover)

The design of a building is a complex process in which spaces are developed which are defined by different parameters. Most important are space requirements, distances, furniture and fittings, and movement zones. Spaces in Architecture is a useful reference work for quickly looking up detailed information and all important dimensions on space scenarios that occur in many different types of buildings.

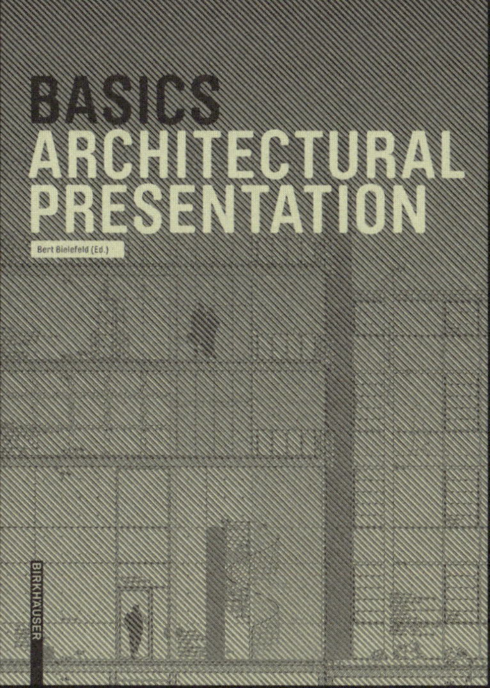

Basics Architectural Presentation

Bert Bielefeld (Ed.)

408 pages, 400 illustrations
978-3-03821-527-1 (Softcover)

First-year students of architecture are confronted with a wealth of different ways in which to present their designs: How to construct a perspective freehand drawing? What scale should a model be? Basics Architectural Presentation combines the volumes Technical Drawing, CAD, Modelbuilding, Architectural Photography, and Freehand Drawing. In a practical approach, it conveys possible ways of presentation throughout the various project phases.

More volumes of the BASICS Student series on birkhauser.com

Designing Cities

Basics, Principles, Projects

Leonhard Schenk

356 pages, 810 illustrations
978-3-0346-1325-5 (Hardcover)

Urban design is based on planning and design principles that need to meet functional demands on the one hand, but on the other hand bring the design elements together into a distinctive whole. Although designs are almost always dominated by the spirit of the times, the basic compositional principles are, for the most part, timeless. Designing Cities examines the most important design and presentation principles of urban design, using selected historical examples and contemporary international competition entries designed by practices including Foster + Partners, KCAP Architects & Planners, MVRDV, and OMA.

Imprint

Concept:
Alexander Schilling, Annette Gref

Translation from German into English:
Raymond Peat

Copy editing:
John O'Toole

Project management:
Annette Gref, Regina Herr

Production:
Heike Strempel

Layout, cover design and typesetting:
Harald Pridgar, Frankfurt/Main

Paper:
Amber Graphic, 120 g/m²

Printing:
Beltz Grafische Betriebe GmbH, Bad Langensalza, Germany

Library of Congress Control Number: 2018949442

Bibliographic information published by the German National Library
The German National Library lists this publication in the Deutsche Nationalbibliografie; detailed bibliographic data are available on the Internet at http://dnb.dnb.de.

ISBN 978-3-0356-1479-4
e-ISBN (PDF) 978-3-0356-1473-2

German Print-ISBN 978-3-0356-1477-0

P.O. Box 44, 4009 Basel, Switzerland
Part of Walter de Gruyter GmbH, Berlin/Boston

9 8 7 6 5 4 3 2 1
www.birkhauser.com